S0-AQG-679

Bowling

SCIENCE BEHIND SPORTS

Bowling

MELISSA ABRAMOVITZ

LUCENT BOOKS

A part of Gale, Cengage Learning

GALE
CENGAGE Learning·

Farmington Hills, Mich • San Francisco • New York • Waterville, Maine
Meriden, Conn • Mason, Ohio • Chicago

© 2015 Gale, Cengage Learning

WCN: 01-100-101

LIBRARY OF CONGRESS CATALOGING-IN-PUBLICATION DATA

Abramovitz, Melissa, 1954-
  Bowling / by Melissa Abramovitz.
    pages cm. -- (Science Behind Sports)
  Includes bibliographical references and index.
  ISBN 978-1-4205-1251-9 (hardcover)
  1. Bowling--Juvenile literature. I. Title.
  GV903.5.A37 2015
  794.6--dc23
                          2014048964

Lucent Books
27500 Drake Rd
Farmington Hills MI 48331

ISBN-13: 978-1-4205-1251-9
ISBN-10: 1-4205-1251-X

Printed in the United States of America
1 2 3 4 5 6 7 19 18 17 16 15

CONTENTS

On March 21, 1970, Slovenian ski jumper Vinko Bogataj took a terrible fall while competing at the Ski-Flying World Championships in Oberstdorf, West Germany. Bogataj's pinwheeling crash was caught on tape by an ABC *Wide World of Sports* film crew and eventually became synonymous with "the agony of defeat" in competitive sporting. While many viewers were transfixed by the severity of Bogataj's accident, most were not aware of the biomechanical and environmental elements behind the skier's fall—heavy snow and wind conditions that made the ramp too fast and Bogataj's inability to maintain his center of gravity and slow himself down. Bogataj's accident illustrates that, no matter how mentally and physically prepared an athlete may be, scientific principles—such as momentum, gravity, friction, and aerodynamics—always have an impact on performance.

Lucent Books' Science Behind Sports series explores these and many more scientific principles behind some of the most popular team and individual sports, including baseball, hockey, gymnastics, wrestling, swimming, and skiing. Each volume in the series focuses on one sport or group of related sports. The volumes open with a brief look at the featured sport's origins, history, and changes, then move on to cover the biomechanics and physiology of playing, related health and medical concerns, and the causes and treatment of sports-related injuries.

In addition to learning about the arc behind a curve ball, the impact of centripetal force on a figure skater, or how water buoyancy helps swimmers, Science Behind Sports readers will also learn how exercise, training, warming up, and diet and nutrition directly relate to peak performance and enjoyment of the sport. Volumes may also cover why certain sports are popular, how sports function in the business world, and which hot sporting issues—sports doping and cheating, for example—are in the news.

Basic physical science concepts, such as acceleration, kinetics, torque, and velocity, are explained in an engaging and accessible manner. The full-color text is augmented by fact boxes, sidebars, photos, and detailed diagrams, charts, and graphs. In addition, a subject-specific glossary, bibliography, and index provide further tools for researching the sports and concepts discussed throughout Science Behind Sports.

CHAPTER 1

Bowling: A Game for All

B owling, which involves knocking down as many pins as possible with a bowling ball, has been enjoyed by people of all ages, athletic abilities, and social classes throughout human history. The American Ten Pins Bowling Association explains that "It is a game that has been played by kings, princes, presidents and the working people of American industry."[1]

As one of the oldest sports known to humankind, bowling continues to enjoy widespread popularity. According to the International Bowling Museum and Hall of Fame, "Bowling has a long and rich history, and today it is one of the most popular sports in the world."[2] About 100 million people in over ninety countries enjoy bowling today, and it is the most popular participatory sport in the United States.

Early Bowling

There is some controversy about exactly when the sport of bowling began, but historians agree that it is one of the oldest sports in the world. Most historians believe people played a bowling-like game as early as 3200 B.C. This belief is based on studies in the 1930s by the British anthropologist Sir Flinders Petrie. Petrie found a stone ball and nine cone-shaped pieces of stone in the tomb of an ancient

Egyptian child. He surmised that the nine stones were set up as pins and the ball was rolled at them in a bowling-like game. Other evidence exists that ancient Egyptians used bowling balls made of corn husks, covered with leather and bound by string, in similar games.

There is a great deal of physical and written evidence that games which involved tossing stone objects at other stone objects were also played in ancient Rome about four thousand years ago. These games were especially popular among soldiers during this era, and they spread throughout the Roman Empire. Various forms of these games, particularly those played in Europe, evolved into modern indoor and outdoor bowling games.

Historians believe the ancestor of the indoor pin bowling games played today in the United States originated in Germany. Bowling historian J. Bruce Pluckhahn explains:

> The modern sport of bowling at pins probably originated in ancient Germany, not as a sport, but as a religious ceremony. As early as the 3rd or 4th century A.D., in rites held in the cloisters of churches, parishioners may have placed their ever-present club, or *Kegel* (the implement most Germans carried for sport and certainly, self-protection), at one end of a runway resembling a modern bowling lane. The *Kegel* was said to represent the *Heide* ("heathen"). A stone was rolled at the *Heide*, and those successfully toppling it were believed to have cleansed themselves of sin.[3]

The ritual became known as kegels or kegeling, and the game of bowling still bears these names in some places today.

Early Variations of Bowling

Over time, the religious ritual of kegels evolved into a social game. For example, historical references to a huge feast given for the citizens of Frankfurt, Germany, in 1463 note that the people bowled after the meal. In 1518 the city of Breslau, Germany, held a bowling tournament. The prize for the winner was an ox. During the 1500s bowling also received much attention in Germany after the clergyman Martin Luther built an indoor bowling lane so his children could play the game. Indoor bowling lanes in Germany were generally made of wood or hardened clay.

Many variations of bowling games developed in other places throughout Europe; some used as few as three pins, while others used as many as seventeen. In England, outdoor lawn bowling became especially popular during the fourteenth century. In fact, it became so popular that King Edward III outlawed the game in 1366 because his soldiers were bowling so much that they skipped their mandatory archery drills. In 1512 King Henry VIII, who was one of many monarchs who enjoyed bowling, again outlawed the sport, but only for the less-well-to-do. He believed working-class people were spending more time bowling than working.

Although outdoor lawn bowling was popular in England, in 1455 the first bowling lanes with roofs appeared in London. This made it possible to bowl in all types of weather, day or night. However, lawn bowling, which

An illustration from a history book published in 1905 depicts Sir Francis Drake in 1588 playing bowls at Plymouth, England, as he is informed that the Spanish Armada is about to invade.

involved rolling large balls and attempting to place them as close as possible to smaller balls called jacks, remained and is still very popular in England. Historical records cite an incident in 1588 as evidence of the extreme popularity of the sport. The British admiral Sir Francis Drake was in the middle of a lawn bowling game when he received word that the Spanish Armada (naval fleet) was close to attacking the British fleet. Drake decided the game was important enough to finish before he led his troops into battle. He famously remarked, "We still have time to finish the game and to thrash the Spaniards, too."[4] Drake lost the game, but he and his soldiers vanquished the Spaniards and won the war.

Bowling in America

During the sixteenth, seventeenth, and eighteenth centuries European immigrants to America brought their own versions of bowling to the new land, and the game became very popular in colonial times. In fact, bowling historian Max Gross writes that "The game of bowling was THE earliest recreational social sport in America."[5] The British settlers in America primarily introduced lawn bowling, while Dutch and German settlers brought their own forms of pin bowling. The Dutch settlers introduced a game that involved rolling the ball along a wooden plank 60 to 90 feet (18 to 27m) long and 12 to 18 inches (30 to 46cm) wide. The target was nine pins set in a diamond-shaped pattern. This game was particularly popular among Dutch settlers in New Amsterdam, which later became New York. An area in the southern part of New York City where settlers played the game became known as Bowling Green and it still bears this name. A similar plank game continues to be played in the Netherlands today.

During the 1700s many Americans bowled outdoors, but bowling gradually became more of an indoor sport modeled on the nine-pin German version of the game. The earliest-known written reference to indoor bowling in the United States appeared in 1819 in author Washington Irving's story "Rip Van Winkle." According to the story, Rip awakened to

Bowling Green is the oldest public park in New York City. It featured a bowling lawn when it was originally built in 1733.

the sound of "crashing ninepins"[6] at nearby bowling lanes. By the 1820s, ninepins, as it was called, was not only widely played, but also became associated with a great deal of gambling and alcohol consumption.

Gambling and alcohol sullied the reputation of ninepins; from the 1820s to 1840s, various communities enacted laws banning ninepins for this reason. For instance, in 1829 the town of Oswego, New York, issued an ordinance stating that bowling lane owner Anson Richardson's ninepin alley was a "public nuisance"[7] and had to be shut down within twenty-four hours. Bowling alley proprietors got around these laws by adding a tenth pin to the game. According to bowling champion and author Parker Bohn III, "Legend has it that a clever and anonymous soul merely added a pin and called the 'new' game bowling."[8] Tenpin bowling became even more popular than ninepins was. By the year 1900, New York City alone had nearly two hundred bowling alleys to accommodate the demand.

Bowling for Laughs and for Charity

The sport of bowling has spurred humorous offshoots such as the Nashville Network television show *Rockin' Bowl*. The show, which aired in 2000, featured collegiate bowlers competing in regular games with a twist—competitors could earn extra points by using some humorous and unconventional techniques. The unconventional techniques included bowling while lying on a hospital gurney, launching the ball with a slingshot, bowling after spinning around, bowling in the dark with glow-in-the-dark pins, bowling while blindfolded, bowling while walking backwards, and disco-bowling with a strobe light.

Rockin' Bowl only ran for about a year, but a modern fundraiser that had nothing to do with the television show adopted the name "Rock 'N' Bowl" for an October 9, 2014, event that featured rock stars and comedians bowling to raise money for cancer research. Among the celebrities were rockers Chris Broderick (Megadeth), Fee Waybill (The Tubes), and John Bush (Armored Saint), and comedians Elayne Boosler, Joe Bartnick, Reggie Brown, and Craig Gass. Many other charitable events have also featured celebrities bowling to raise money for worthy causes.

Although gambling and drinking alcohol persisted in the new game of tenpins, two factors that helped counterbalance the game's poor reputation were that many wealthy people began building bowling lanes in their mansions and that many prominent individuals enjoyed the sport. In 1860, for example, Prince Albert Edward of Britain visited the United States and Canada and was introduced to bowling at the homes of several wealthy families. The prince greatly enjoyed the sport, and numerous mentions of this in newspapers provided a positive boost for bowling's reputation.

This kind of publicity helped bowling become a popular family sport even though it remained associated with gambling and drinking in some areas.

President Abraham Lincoln also enjoyed bowling and promoted the game. Later on, Presidents Harry Truman and Ronald Reagan, baseball star Babe Ruth, and actors Bob Hope and Mickey Rooney were among the celebrities who increased public interest in the game. Truman even had two bowling lanes installed in the White House basement.

Uniform Rules and Widepread Popularity

As bowling became more and more popular throughout the United States, tournaments were organized in many localities. But as Pluckhahn notes, "Although intercity bowling events were becoming common, the lack of uniform playing rules and equipment specifications stifled the development of the game."[9] Since the rules varied from place to place, it was impossible to hold national tournaments. In 1875 nine bowling clubs in New York City founded the National Bowling Association to establish common standards, but disagreements over which rules to adopt prevented this organization from achieving its goals.

In 1895, however, a group of bowling enthusiasts founded the American Bowling Congress (ABC). The new organization managed to develop national rules and equipment standards. For instance, rules mandated that bowling pins should not be more than 15 inches (38cm) tall, which remains the maximum height today. Other rules that still exist include allowing each player two throws per frame and placing the headpin (the front-most pin) 60 feet (18m) from the foul line. A frame is a set of ten pins; the term is also used to refer to one turn (which consists of two throws) in a bowling game. The foul line is a line drawn

on the boards at the end of the approach area to the lane. Players must remain behind the foul line when they throw the ball. Another rule that still exists is that a perfect score of 300 is achieved by bowling twelve consecutive strikes. A strike is achieved when a player knocks down all the pins on the first throw of a frame. When a player topples all the pins in two throws, this is called a spare.

In 1901 the ABC organized the first national bowling tournament. Forty-one men's teams competed in this tournament for the prize of $1,200, which was a substantial sum of money in those days. The first national women's bowling tournament occurred in 1907 in St. Louis, and in 1916 a group of women bowlers founded the Women's International Bowling Congress. This organization began hosting annual national championships for women. During the early 1900s bowling was indeed one of the few sports considered to be acceptable for women.

Fans watch the American Bowling Congress tournament in 1905.

Bumper Bowling

In 1982 the invention of bumper bowling helped make bowling the family sport it is today. Zena Sheinberg (a special education teacher) and Alex Wortman (a social worker) of Ann Arbor, Michigan, took a group of mentally impaired students to a bowling center and noticed most of the balls ended up in the gutters. They came up with the idea of blocking the gutters to keep the ball on the lane, experimenting with long cardboard tubes and other types of tubes. Sheinberg told the *Los Angeles Times*, "Once we figured out a way to make the ball continue down the lane, the kids started having fun."[1] Sheinberg and Wortman eventually obtained a patent for inflatable bumper tubes made of waterbed fabric, and a company called DBA began manufacturing and selling the product. Bowling lane proprietors and parents loved the bumpers because they helped young children learn to bowl. After this, bowling birthday parties and similar family events became popular.

In the late 1980s, Dallas bowling lane owner Phil Kinzer helped two engineers develop a retractable rail system that allowed lane operators to raise and lower the bumpers without having to inflate and deflate them every time they were used. This system began selling around 1990. According to an article on the About Sports website, the rail system and bumpers were "a very important innovation and a main reason bowling is the top recreational sport in America."[2]

1. Quoted in Joan Libman. "Keeping Kids Out of the Gutter: Bumper Bowling Gives Youngsters Respectable Scores." *Los Angeles Times*, September 11, 1988. http://articles.latimes.com/1988-09-11/news/vw-2566_1_bumper-bowling.

2. Jef Goodger. "Bumper Bowling." About Sports. http://bowling.about.com/od/bowlingcenters/qt/Bumper-Bowling.htm.

Gradually, standardized rules led bowling to become a competitive sport not just for amateurs, but also for professionals, who earned their living by bowling in tournaments. In 1958 the founding of the Professional Bowler's Association of America (PBA) and comparable organizations in other countries led to bowling being recognized as an international professional sport whose competitors could earn healthy prize money. The PBA Tour started in 1959 with three tournaments worth $29,500 combined. By 1963, the Tour included thirty-eight tournaments worth a total of $1 million. Today, each tournament can be worth anywhere from $100,000 to $1,000,000.

Equipment Advances

As the sport of bowling advanced with standardized rules, improvements in bowling equipment also fueled its popularity. Several inventions made returning bowling balls and setting up and removing pins faster and easier. Until the 1940s, workers known as pinboys set up and removed pins after they were knocked down in bowling alleys. Pinboys also walked bowling balls back to bowlers after each turn. During the 1700s, lane builders began adding gutters at the sides of the lanes. This allowed pinboys to roll the ball back to bowlers. In 1907 an invention called the automatic pinsetter, or pinspotter, made pinboys' job even easier. Rather than having to manually reset the pins after each shot, the automatic pinsetter allowed pinboys to place the pins into a triangular rack that they lowered by pulling a lever.

A group of men is trained on the workings of an automatic bowling pin resetting machine in 1961.

Many bowlers and bowling lane owners, however, wanted a completely automatic method of removing and

setting pins. This was in large part because many pin-boys were not honest. During the 1920s to 1940s pin-boys were paid about five cents per game. According to bowling champion Joe Norris, who was a pinboy before he became a champion, this low rate of pay motivated many pinboys (not Norris) to cheat for bowlers who paid them bribes. The boys would sneakily kick over an extra pin or two while placing the pins in the automatic pinsetter after the bowler's first throw, making it easier for the bribers to make a spare. Being aware of this practice, Norris was on the lookout for cheating pinboys when he became a competitive bowler. The book *Bowling: How to Master the Game* reveals that "When competing, Joe Norris made it a point to station a friend behind the pin deck to make certain that when his opponent shot the laws of gravity weren't violated by a pinboy whose greased palm inspired soccerlike skills."[10]

One New York lane owner named George Beckerle was especially frustrated with these practices and came up with an idea for a mechanical pinsetter and pin remover. Several people set to work trying to develop such a machine. In 1944 Gottfried Schmidt of New York registered a patent for his automatic pinsetter. It took several more years to make the machine work properly, but once it was perfected, many bowling lane owners purchased the devices, and pinboys were no longer needed. The new machines made games move faster because there was no need to wait while pin-boys picked up and placed pins in racks.

Another technical innovation made it easier to determine whether competitive bowlers stepped over the foul line (which was against the rules and disqualified the throw). Previously, tournament judges made this decision based on sight, but in 1939 the Luxor Bowl in Los Angeles introduced the first electric foul light and buzzer that were activated when someone stepped over the foul line.

Bowling Ball Innovations

Advances also occurred in bowling balls. By the 1800s most bowlers used wooden balls, usually made of a hardwood

called lignum vitae. During the early 1900s hard rubber balls with a thumbhole and one finger hole for the middle finger were introduced. In the 1930s an engineer and recreational bowler named Sully Bates came up with the idea of adding a third hole to these balls after he noticed that a woman with whom he was bowling had difficulties holding onto the ball. Bates realized that adding a hole for the ring finger and drilling the thumbhole at an angle would allow people with small hands to easily hold the ball. His innovation became known as the Bates grip, and soon three-holed balls were standard.

Innovations also occurred in bowling ball coverstocks (coverings) and cores (centers). By the late 1950s balls were

Controversies About Bowling Balls

The covering layers, or coverstocks, on modern high-tech bowling balls have contributed to dramatic increases in scores because they grip the lane and help the ball curve. In 1974, for instance, American Bowling Congress members rolled 1,377 perfect scores of three hundred. In 1999 this number rose to 34,470, and since then it has increased even more. Increased scores have led to controversies about the integrity of the sport. Experts worry that if everyone can get a perfect score, the game is no longer challenging or competitive. As United States Bowling Congress (USBC) technical director Neil Stremmel explains, "USBC is concerned that technology has overtaken player skill in determining success in the sport of bowling." USBC, which regulates bowling rules and equipment standards, therefore performed a study that was completed in 2007 to determine whether new equipment regulations were needed. The study led the USBC to implement new rules about acceptable ball surfaces to help insure that player skill still determines players' scores.

Bowling Digital. "Research Complete on USBC Bowling Ball Motion Study." December 18, 2007. www.bowlingdigital.com/bowl/node/3473.

covered with hard polyester. In the 1980s polyurethane covers were introduced; reactive resin covers followed in the 1990s, and particle-enhanced resin debuted in the early twenty-first century. Ball covers greatly influence how the ball rolls and curves. So do cores, which evolved from simple weight blocks to various combinations of metal, plastic, or ceramic blocks with varying shapes, from oblong to lightbulb-shaped. The weight, shape, and placement of the core affect the ball's path, rotation, and speed. Today, most elite bowlers invest in custom-made, technologically-superior balls that can cost several hundred dollars each.

Most of these bowlers have four or more different balls to use for different lane conditions.

Bowling Remains Popular

Between improvements in bowling balls and the use of automatic pinsetters, the popularity of bowling in the United States soared and the number of bowling lanes tripled between the 1940s and the 1960s. Although the number of people participating in bowling leagues peaked during the 1960s, the game remains very popular at the recreational and competitive levels. Today, over 70 million people bowl at least once a year in the United States. Tenpin bowling is the most prevalent form of the game in America, but other forms such as duckpins, candlepins, and ninepins are played in some locations. Candlepins is mostly played in parts of Canada and in New England. It uses smaller balls than tenpins and the balls have no holes. The pins are thinner and harder to knock down. Duckpins also uses smaller balls, but uses shorter, fatter pins than tenpins.

Today, many nations have national bowling organizations that set rules and standards. The Fédération Internationale des Quilleurs is the international governing organization for worldwide competitions. In the United States, the United States Bowling Congress (USBC), founded in 2005 to replace several national organizations like the ABC, oversees rules and policies.

Although bowling is an international sport and many bowlers and bowling advocates have tried to get it approved as an Olympic sport, thus far this has not happened, though it was featured as an exhibition sport in the 1936 and 1988 Olympic Games. Bowling is, however, a World Cup sport and is widely viewed throughout the world on television. Its popularity as a televised sport began in the 1960s when bowling shows such as *Championship Bowling*, *Bowling for Dollars*, and *Jackpot Bowling* debuted. Bowling is

KINGPIN

4,061

The number of bowling centers in the United States in 2012

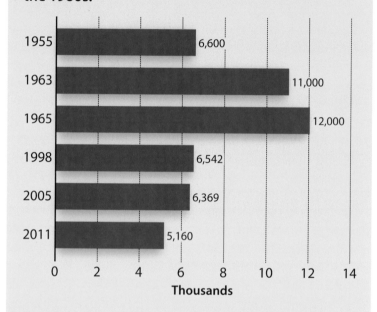

NUMBER OF BOWLING CENTERS IN THE UNITED STATES

Bowling increased rapidly in popularity in the middle of the twentieth century. By the early twenty-first century, the number of bowling centers was about half the number at its peak in the 1960s.

Year	Number
1955	6,600
1963	11,000
1965	12,000
1998	6,542
2005	6,369
2011	5,160

Thousands

Source: John McDuling. "Let the Good Times Roll: The Incredible Bowling Bubble of the 1960s," *The Atlantic*, March 28, 2014. www.theatlantic.com/technology/archive/2014/03/let-the-good-times-roll-the-incredible-bowling-bubble-of-the-1960s/359787.

also featured in many movies, such as *The Odd Couple; Girl, Interrupted;* and *Kingpin*, as an intricate part of American culture.

While bowling remains popular for spectators, most people who spend time at bowling alleys do so to play the game, either as a recreational sport, in leagues and other amateur competitions, or as professionals. Bowling is also a popular high school and collegiate sport; the USBC notes that it is one of the fastest-growing high school sports in the twenty-first century. In 2014 about five thousand high schools in the United States had boys and girls bowling teams.

Numerous experts have noted that bowling is indeed well-suited for people of all ages, social classes, and athletic abilities, making it an ideal universal sport. As *Buzzle* journalist Earl Hunsinger writes in an article titled "Bowling: The Sport of Kings and Working Men," "It's fascinating to know that it was once the sport of kings. Yet, that's not why we go bowling. We bowl because it's enjoyable and gives us a chance to relax and spend time with our family and friends."[11]

CHAPTER 2

Physics and Bowling

Whether people bowl for recreation or competition, the sport involves numerous scientific principles that influence the motion of the bowler, the ball, and the pins in relation to the bowling lanes. Two of the main areas of science that apply to bowling are physics and biomechanics. Physics describes and explains the properties and relationships between physical objects. Biomechanics is the study of how the laws of physics and mechanics affect the ways in which the human body moves.

Forces of Nature

The laws of physics that apply to bowling describe and explain how forces control bowling balls, pins, and interactions between the ball, the bowler, and the lane. A force is a source of energy that pushes or pulls an object. Scientists measure forces in units called newtons. The newton is named after the English physicist and mathematician Sir Isaac Newton, whose work in the seventeenth century provided the foundation for modern physical sciences.

The amount of force needed to speed up (accelerate) something weighing 1 kilogram at a rate of 1 meter per second squared equals 1 newton. For example, a 1-liter bottle of water weighs 1 kilogram. A person would have to push on the bottle with 1 newton of force to make it accelerate at a rate of 1 meter per second squared. This is not a lot of force; most humans can exert up to around 675 newtons of force. A boxer's punch, on the other hand, can generate up to around 5,000 newtons.

Many forces interact to produce and modify the motions that underlie bowling. These include forces an athlete's movements impose on a bowling ball, forces the environment applies to athletes and the ball, and forces the ball applies to the pins. These forces can be internal or external, and multiple forces can act on a person or object. Internal forces are those created inside an individual's body by muscles and bones, or inside a bowling ball by its core. External forces come from outside the person or object being acted upon. External forces can be applied directly

A bowling ball's movement from a bowler to the pins—the basis of the sport—is the result of the interactions of a number of internal and external forces.

through contact or at a distance. An example of a contact force is the force between a bowling ball and the pins it strikes. One force which acts at a distance (known as a field force) is the force of gravity. Gravity pulls objects to the earth's surface.

If an object is at rest, the sum of the contact and field forces acting on it is zero. In order for an object to move, one or multiple forces must start this motion. The total, or net, forces acting on the object determine the speed, distance, and direction the object travels.

Newton's Laws of Motion

Newton's laws of motion describe and explain how forces influence motion. Newton's first law states that an object at rest will remain at rest and an object in motion will remain in motion unless an outside force acts to change its velocity. Velocity is a measurement of how fast an object is changing its original position. This differs from speed, which only measures the distance an object moves in a certain amount of time. Velocity measures both speed and direction. Basically, Newton's first law means that "there is a natural tendency of objects to keep on doing what they're doing."[12] In bowling, Newton's first law indicates that bowling pins will remain at rest until the ball strikes them, which provides the force to move them. At the same, the law indicates that the bowling ball will keep moving at the same speed and in the same direction until the pins blocking its path cause it to change its velocity.

The principles of physics that underlie Newton's first law are inertia and momentum. Inertia is the tendency of an object at rest to stay at rest and of an object in motion to remain in motion. Inertia increases as an object's mass increases; that is, more force is required to move a more massive object from its resting position or to change its velocity when in motion. Thus, it takes more force to move a car

than a penny because the car has more mass. Mass is a measurement of how much matter an object contains. Mass differs from weight, which depends on the amount of gravity pushing on the object. An object's mass is the same on the earth as it is in a place that has less gravity, such as the moon, but an object weighs less in places where there is less gravity.

Momentum is related to inertia. Momentum describes the direction and speed of a moving object relative to its mass—the momentum of an object equals its mass times its velocity. When moving at the same velocity, a more massive object thus has more momentum than a less massive one. Because of its momentum, the more massive object, such as a car, needs more force to slow or stop it than a less massive one, such as a bicycle.

Newton's second law of motion also involves momentum and inertia. The second law explains how an object's velocity changes when forces are applied to overcome its inertia. It states that an object's acceleration is directly proportional to the total external forces acting on it and inversely proportional to the object's mass. This means that the more force is applied, the faster the object will accelerate, except

Newton's laws of motion are basic principles that describe how all objects—including bowling balls and pins—move.

that more massive objects do not accelerate as quickly as less massive ones do. Thus, a 16-pound (7-kg) bowling ball does not accelerate as fast as a 10-pound (5-kg) ball when the same amount of force is applied.

Newton's third law explains how the forces that act on objects interact. It states that every action creates an opposite and equally forceful reaction. As an article on the Live Science website explains, "Forces always occur in pairs; when one body pushes against another, the second body pushes back just as hard."[13] For instance, a bowler exerts force on the floor on which he stands, and the floor exerts an equal and opposite force on the bowler. The force the ground exerts on people or objects is called the ground reaction force.

Bowling and Newton's Laws

Newton's laws apply to many aspects of bowling. For example, since force is needed to overcome an object's inertia, according to Newton's first law, bowlers learn to transfer the momentum from a moving arm and shoulder to a bowling ball to start it rolling. Bowlers also try to impart the maximum speed to the ball when they release it because "The faster the speed of the rolling ball is, the more momentum there will be"[14] and the more pins will fall, according to an article titled "The Physics of Bowling." The speed at which bowlers release the ball varies widely, but experts consider a speed of less than 17 miles per hour (27 kmh) to be slow and one of greater than 19 miles per hour (31 kmh) to be fast. Also according to Newton's first law, once the ball is in motion, it stays in motion until outside forces, such as hitting the pins, act to slow or stop it. Newton's second law also applies to the ball hitting the pins. A heavier ball hits the pins with more force than a lighter one, since force equals mass times acceleration.

One way in which Newton's third law affects bowling is that bowlers take several steps before releasing the ball to influence the ball's motion. When someone stands still, she exerts a force on the ground equal to her weight, and the ground exerts an equal and opposite force on her. But when she moves, her feet press against the ground intermittently,

Spin, Gravity, and Bowling Balls

The spin a bowler puts on a bowling ball not only affects its path, but also influences how gravity acts on it as it falls to the ground. Laws of physics called the Magnus effect and Bernoulli's principle govern the way in which spin affects an object. The Swiss mathematician Daniel Bernoulli first demonstrated the principle that bears his name in the 1700s. It states that the faster air moves over or around an object, the less pressure the air puts on the object. The Magnus effect was named for the German chemist and physicist Gustav Magnus after he demonstrated the principle in 1852. It states that a spinning object changes its path through the air according to the direction of the spin. This occurs because the pressure of the air moving around a moving object is equal on all sides when the object is not spinning, but adding spin changes this pressure. Most bowlers add topspin to the ball. Topspin causes the top of the ball to move in the direction opposite to the direction of the airflow around it. At the same time, the bottom moves in the same direction as the air. The opposing motion on the top creates drag (increased air resistance). Drag makes the air move slowly over the top and faster over the bottom. The slower-moving air over the top puts more pressure on the ball, according to Bernoulli's principle. This creates the Magnus effect that pushes the ball downward faster than gravity alone would push it.

and this changes the ground reaction force. The ground reaction force increases as she presses harder and faster on the floor, and this force can be transferred to the ball to give it more power.

Energy and Gravity

The forces described by Newton's laws relate closely to the concepts of energy and work. According to the Institute of

Physics, a force is a "mechanism by which energy is transferred from one body to another. . . . Work is done by a force when the object concerned moves in the direction of the force, and the force thereby transfers energy from one object to another."[15] Energy is defined as the capacity of a person or object to do work or cause a change in something. Bowlers transfer energy from their muscles and from the force of gravity to the ball to make it move.

The force of gravity and its relationship to potential (stored) energy and kinetic (moving) energy are extremely important in bowling. Bowlers use gravity to power the arm swing they use to launch the ball. As a bowler holds the ball at the top of the arm swing, it has gravitational potential energy (GPE) because of its position off the ground. In other words, the ball has the potential to fall to the ground from the force of gravity. The higher the bowler holds the ball, the more potential energy it has because more work was done to lift it higher up. The amount of GPE equals an object's mass times gravitational acceleration times how high the object is off the ground. Gravitational acceleration is

A bowler uses energy to counteract the gravitational force on the ball and lift it. Gravitational energy also plays a role in the ball's acceleration when the bowler releases it.

Factors That Affect Bowling Ball Motion

A 2007 study by the United States Bowling Congress (USBC) measured which factors most influence bowling ball motion. Researchers placed twenty-three sensors hooked up to a computer system called SuperCATS next to a lane to measure ball position, velocity, and vertical angle as a ball rolled down the lane. They also programmed a robot named Harry to throw different balls with exactly the same path, the same speed of 17 miles per hour (27 kmh), and the same spin rate of 275 revolutions per minute. These values mimic how an average advanced adult bowler throws the ball.

Experts divide bowling ball motion into three phases. In the skid phase the ball slides in a straight line because it has not yet been affected by enough friction to hook. In the hook phase it begins curving. In the roll phase it again rolls straight. The researchers found the main factors affecting this motion are the ball's cover, the coefficient of friction between the ball and lane, how fast the ball absorbs oil, the radius of gyration, and the rate of revolution. They concluded that "technological advances in bowling ball coverstocks and cores have increased the complexity of the physics of bowling ball motion on a bowling lane."

Neil Stremmel, Paul Ridenour, and Scott Sterbenz. "Identifying the Critical Factors That Contribute to Bowling Ball Motion on a Bowling Lane." http://usbcongress .http.internapcdn.net/usbcongress/bowl/equipandspecs/pdfs/BallMotionASQ.pdf.

the amount that gravity causes objects to accelerate towards the earth's surface. This amount is 9.8 meters per second squared (32.17 feet/sec squared). The higher the object is, the more it accelerates when it drops, since it is in the air longer.

A bowling ball's GPE is converted to kinetic energy after gravity pulls the ball to the bottom of the arm swing arc and the bowler releases it. Gravity also pulls the ball to the ground after the release and keeps it there. As it begins rolling, the kinetic energy of the ball equals its mass times its velocity squared, divided by two ($KE = mv^2/2$). Thus, a heavier ball moves down a lane with more energy than a lighter ball does.

The combined potential and kinetic energy an object possesses is known as its mechanical energy. The mechanical energy of an object can change between kinetic and potential forms, but the total amount of energy is conserved (stays the same). Thus, as a bowling ball goes through a bowler's arm swing, the amount of potential and kinetic energy change, but the total mechanical energy is conserved.

Frictional Forces

Once a bowling ball hits the lane and starts rolling, other forces begin to influence its motion and speed. One such force is friction, which occurs when two objects come in contact. As the article "The Physics of Bowling" explains, "After the ball is released, it slows down due to friction between the ball and the lane. On average, 3 mph [5 kmh] is lost during the time the ball rolls down the 60 foot [18m] lane."[16] Some friction is desirable in bowling because friction allows the ball to curve, or hook, which increases the chances of achieving a strike. But too much friction can slow the ball down too much and deplete some of its energy, so bowlers combine proper technique with selecting a ball whose coverstock produces the ideal amount of friction for particular lane conditions.

There are several types of friction. The type that has the most effect on bowling is contact friction, also called dry or sliding friction. Contact friction exists whether or not an object is moving. When two objects in contact are motionless, physicists say that static friction exists. When one or both are moving, kinetic friction exists between them.

Even smooth objects exert contact friction on each other because microscopic peaks and valleys in the surfaces catch on each other and form molecular bonds. Physics professor John Goff explains in his book *Gold Medal Physics: The Science of Sports* that these bonds help explain the differences between static and kinetic friction: "As two objects

Bowling Ball Grit

A bowling ball that hooks correctly hits the pins accurately and forcefully. Without friction, hooking does not happen, so modern reactive resin balls offer a range of coverstocks that can be sanded to influence the ball's friction with the lane. A bowler's bowling style, along with lane oil conditions, help determine which coverstock is ideal for a particular situation.

The main types of coverstocks are solid, pearlized, and hybrid. The smoothness of the ball's surface is called its grit. Grits values range from 180 to 4,000. The lower the grit number is, the rougher is the surface texture. Solid covers have a lightly-sanded matte finish with a low grit. They are usually used on lanes with medium to large amounts of oil. Their low grit gives the ball a high coefficient of friction, so it grabs the lane and hooks sooner. Balls with solid covers thus lose more speed than those with pearlized covers, which are smoother and have a lower coefficient of friction. Pearlized covers allow the ball to roll further before hooking, so its momentum builds up longer and is released primarily at the end of the lane near the pins. Pearlized covers are generally used on drier lanes. Hybrid covers are a cross between solid and pearlized covers.

slide against each other, bonds are continually broken and remade. The bonds made during sliding are not as "tight" as those made when the surfaces are at rest with respect to each other, thus explaining qualitatively why static friction is usually greater in magnitude than kinetic friction."[17]

The two objects' weights and surface qualities determine how much friction holds back the sliding motion and also influence the amount of external force that must be applied to overcome static and kinetic friction. Heavier objects and those with rough surfaces press more tightly against each other, so the amount of friction between them is greater. Scientists call the amount of force needed to overcome the

300 revolutions per minute

The rate at which an average bowler can make a bowling ball spin

friction between two objects the coefficient of friction.

Coefficients of friction exist for both static and kinetic friction. The coefficient of static friction is the amount of force needed to start a nonmoving object moving over another object. The coefficient of kinetic friction is the amount of force needed to keep one object sliding over the other at a constant speed. The coefficient of static friction for two blocks of glass, for example, is 0.94. This means a force equal to 94 percent of the object's weight is needed to start it sliding over the other object. The coefficient of kinetic friction is 0.40. The coefficient of static friction is greater than the coefficient of kinetic friction because it takes more force to overcome inertia than momentum. Most dry surfaces have coefficients of kinetic friction between 0.3 and 0.6; though if one surface is rubber, the coefficients usually range from one to two. Regulations mandate that the coefficient of kinetic friction for a bowling ball must not exceed 0.32.

Friction between two surfaces converts some kinetic energy into heat and also wears down the surfaces. This is the main reason why oil is applied to bowling lanes—to cut down on the lanes' wear and tear. The addition of oil to bowling lanes reduces the sliding friction between the ball and lanes because of the addition of a lubricating layer of liquid. Thus, the motion of a bowling ball includes another type of friction called lubricated friction. Some bowling lanes have more oil than others, and these lanes create less friction, so the ball slows down and curves less. The ball's coverstock also affects lubricated friction. Reactive resin covers absorb more oil and create more friction between the ball and the lane than plastic covers do.

Rotation and Revolution

Friction and lane oil affect the path and spin of a bowling ball as well as its speed. Good bowlers put spin on the

TORQUE AND ROTATION

Torque is the force that causes the bowling ball to rotate on an axis. The friction of the bowling lane causes resistance that keeps the ball from sliding, though the oil on lanes may reduce this friction, allowing the ball to slide.

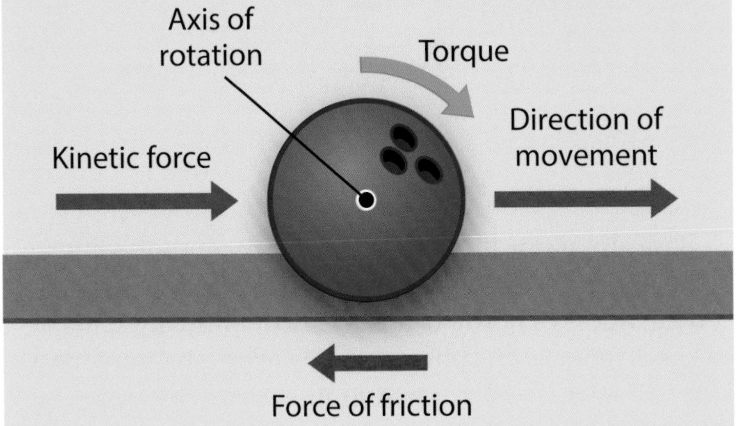

Axis of rotation

Torque

Direction of movement

Kinetic force

Force of friction

ball and often make it hook, so laws of physics pertaining to rotation and revolution also apply to bowling. Bowling balls rotate and revolve. Revolutions refer to the number of times the ball turns over, also known as the ball's rev rate. Rotation is the angle at which the ball revolves. A bowling ball's rotation and revolution are determined partly by how the bowler turns his wrist when releasing the ball. The turn of the wrist imparts torque to the ball. Torque is a measurement of how much force acting on an object causes the object to rotate. This is determined by the angle at which the force is applied and the distance of the object from the force. Adding torque to a bowling ball is one factor that increases the force with which it hits the pins.

Rotation, revolution, and torque also affect how the ball curves. The book *Bowler's Handbook: A Guide to Almost Everything in Bowling* explains how these concepts relate to friction and lane oil:

Bowling lanes are shiny because they are lubricated with oil to reduce friction. The lubrication also affects how the bowling balls rotate and spin.

Basically, a bowling ball rotates, rolls, and/or spins in a certain direction on its path or trajectory to a target. Regardless of how a ball is released, it usually spins or slides in the initial phases after its release because most bowling lanes are covered in mineral oil over the first 30 to 40 feet [9 to 12m]. When the ball eventually grips the lane, [the ball's trajectory] will follow the rotation of the ball. If the rotation is strong and horizontal, the ball will hook.[18]

Another factor that affects a bowling ball's circular motion is its radius of gyration (RG). RG describes how the mass of the weight block that sits inside all bowling balls is distributed. RG numbers vary from 2.48 to 2.80. The weight block in balls with a lower RG sits near the center. This means the ball will start to spin sooner and faster than one with higher RG, where the mass is closer to the edges. One method of picturing this principle is to imagine an ice skater spinning. She spins faster if her arms are held close to her body than if the arms are extended.

Because it rotates and revolves, a bowling ball has angular momentum in addition to forward momentum. This means it goes forward, but is also pulled sideways by its rotation. The amount of angular momentum equals the ball's angular velocity times its moment of inertia. Angular velocity is the rate at which the object is rotating. The moment of inertia measures how an object's mass influences its resistance to changes in its angular velocity. A bowling ball's angular momentum is important because it affects the force with which it hits the pins.

Crashing Tenpins

When the ball collides with the pins, its forward and angular momentum are transferred to the pins because the principle of conservation of momentum states that collisions

Bowlers apply the scientific principles of motion every time they bowl a strike.

between hard objects conserve momentum. The ball loses momentum and the pins gain momentum during the collision, but the total amount of momentum stays the same. However, not all of the ball's kinetic energy is transferred to the pins because the collision is both elastic and inelastic. Elastic collisions involve no loss of kinetic energy, while part of the kinetic energy in inelastic collisions is changed to another form of energy, such as heat or sound (as in the crashing sound heard when a bowling ball hits the pins). The book *Matter and Interactions* explains that "With macroscopic systems there are no perfectly elastic collisions, because there is always some dissipation [loss]"[19] of kinetic energy. The fact that the ball and pins come to rest after the collision also shows that the collision is partly inelastic. In a perfectly elastic collision, the objects keep moving. In a perfectly inelastic collision, the colliding objects stick together.

Bowlers use the principles governing the motion of colliding objects, friction, and other laws of physics every time they bowl. They learn to apply forces from their muscles to the ball in ways that maximize the accuracy and power of their shots so as to topple as many pins as possible. The ways in which they do this are explained by the science of kinesiology (movement) and its subfield of biomechanics.

CHAPTER 3

Biomechanics and Bowling

The principles of physics and mechanics that apply to bowling ball motion also apply to bowlers' motions. As kinesiology expert Carol Oatis explains in *Kinesiology: The Mechanics and Pathomechanics of Human Movement*, "Although the human body is an incredibly complex biological system composed of trillions of cells, it is subject to the same fundamental laws of mechanics that govern simple metal or plastic structures."[20] The ability to perform the skills required for bowling depends on bowlers training various parts of the body to work in harmony with these laws of physics and biomechanics. Training involves practicing these skills, along with strengthening and conditioning the body so it can execute the skills effectively and consistently.

Muscle Matters

All sports skills depend on using and coordinating the muscles that control movement. Bowling uses muscles throughout the body, from the large quadriceps muscles in the legs to small finger muscles. The human body contains three types of muscles: smooth, cardiac, and skeletal. Smooth muscles are found in organs and blood vessels throughout the body. Cardiac muscle allows the heart to pump blood. Both smooth and cardiac muscles operate involuntarily; that is, they do not require an individual's conscious control. On the other hand, skeletal, or striated, muscles are under voluntary control. Skeletal muscles are connected to bones (the skeleton) with cartilage structures called tendons. Muscles cause bones to move by pulling on these tendons and on the ligaments that connect bones to each other. The human body has 206 bones; 177 of these bones engage in voluntary movements. The bones that do not move the body are the flat bones, such as the skull and ribcage, which exist to protect internal organs.

All muscles consist of elastic tissue that stretches and contracts (shortens) to move different body parts. This elastic tissue is made up of bundles of cells called muscle fiber cells, or myocytes. Each myocyte contains many strands of protein called myofibrils. Myofibril strands contain filaments made of the proteins actin and myosin. Actin filaments are about seven nanometers in diameter; myosin filaments are about fifteen nanometers. In comparison, one human hair is sixty to eighty thousand nanometers wide. One nanometer is one-billionth of a meter. Myosin filaments grab onto actin filaments by forming chemical bonds known as crossbridges, then pull the actin filaments past them. This shortens the myofibril. When many myofibrils inside many myocytes shorten, entire muscles contract. Muscles stretch when myofibrils return to their original position.

It is these skeletal muscle stretches and contractions that make voluntary motions, such as throwing a bowling ball, possible. Oatis explains that "Skeletal muscle is a fascinating biological tissue able to transform chemical energy to mechanical energy. . . . The production of movement and force is the mechanical outcome of skeletal muscle contraction."[21]

Aristotle and Biomechanics

Kinesiology and biomechanics were not recognized as formal scientific disciplines until the twentieth century. However, scientists and philosophers throughout history, such as Aristotle, Leonardo da Vinci, and Galileo Galilei, discussed the ways in which the laws of physics and mechanics apply to living creatures. For example, in 350 B.C. the Greek philosopher/scientist Aristotle wrote in his treatise *On the Gait of Animals*:

> Now of animals which change their position some move with the whole body at once, for example, jumping animals, others move one part first and then the other, for example walking (and running) animals. In both these changes the moving creature always changes its position by pressing against what lies beneath it. . . . [A]n animal which jumps makes its jump both by leaning against its own upper part and also against what is beneath its feet; for at the joints the parts do in a sense lean upon one another, and in general that which pushes down leans upon what is pushed down.

In this section of the treatise Aristotle described what later became Newton's third law of motion and the biomechanical principles of how muscles and bones exert forces to move living creatures.

Aristotle. *On the Gait of Animals*. Translated by A.S.L. Farquharson. http://classics.mit.edu/Aristotle/gait_anim.html.

Muscle Fuel

Human muscles contain two types of muscle fibers—slow-twitch (ST), or type 1, fibers and fast-twitch (FT), or type 2, fibers—which generate the fuel that lets them turn chemical energy into the energy of motion. The fuel is called adenosine triphosphate (ATP). FT fibers produce ATP anaerobically, meaning without oxygen, using two types of anaerobic chemical reactions. The first type involves converting phosphocreatine into ATP. Muscle cells

A balanced diet includes the protein, fats, and carbohydrates the body needs for energy and to replenish muscle cells.

store phosphocreatine, which is a chemical they get from food. But phosphocreatine only provides enough ATP to last about ten seconds. When muscles need energy for more than ten seconds, FT fibers use glycolysis to generate this energy. Glycolysis burns glucose (sugar in the blood) or glycogen (sugar stored in the liver). Glycolysis can be sustained for about two minutes. These processes make FT fibers ideal for generating short bursts of strength or speed. If more energy is needed, the aerobic energy system that involves ST fibers taking oxygen from the blood becomes active. ST fibers make ATP by burning both fat and glucose in a chemical reaction that requires oxygen. Aerobic ATP production can be sustained for long periods of time. It thus allows ST fibers to keep converting ATP into the mechanical energy needed for activities such as distance running.

The transformation of ATP to mechanical energy follows a law of physics called the first law of thermodynamics. According to NASA (the National Aeronautics and Space Administration), "Thermodynamics is a branch of physics which deals with the energy and work of a system."[22] The first law of thermodynamics states that energy cannot be created, but can be transformed from one form to another. Muscle fibers are designed to transform the oxygen taken into the body by the lungs and the nutrients taken from foods in a person's diet into chemical energy in the form of ATP. They then transform ATP into movement.

Muscle fibers thus depend on receiving adequate nutrition and adequate amounts of oxygen to function. This is one reason that exercise physiologists emphasize the importance of eating a healthy diet. A well-balanced diet contains the protein, fats, and carbohydrates needed for cell growth, upkeep, and energy production. Proteins, which come from meats, dairy products, eggs, nuts, legumes, and some vegetables, mainly provide the chemicals needed to repair body tissues. Cells convert carbohydrates, found in pasta, rice, whole grains, vegetables, and fruits, into glucose. Fats come from oils and many protein sources. According to the National Institutes of Health, "Nutrition can help enhance athletic performance. . . . Eating a good diet can help provide the energy you need to finish a race, or just enjoy a casual sport or activity. You are more likely to be tired and perform poorly during sports when you do not get enough calories, carbohydrates, fluids, iron, vitamins, and other minerals, [and] protein."[23]

Careers in Sports Science

People interested in a career relating to sports sciences can choose from many specialties. A career in biomechanics, which is a sub-discipline of kinesiology, may include working as a trainer, coach, physical therapist, researcher, sports medicine expert, or teacher. Biomechanics experts can also become engineers who design machines and devices that help athletes perform or that help people with disabilities move around. Experts in sports sciences can also be medical doctors who specialize in sports medicine or psychologists who specialize in sports psychology.

People with sports science careers usually have undergraduate or graduate degrees in math, physics, physiology, kinesiology, medicine, psychology, or engineering. These types of degrees allow sports scientists to specialize in any of the many aspects of training, healing, motivating, and teaching people who participate in sports.

Motor Units

Although muscle fibers generate the energy needed for movement, they could not operate without instructions from nerve cells, or neurons, in the brain and spinal cord. When

KINGPIN

Bowling uses every major muscle group in the human body.

an individual wants to move a body part, neurons in the brain send chemical and electrical messages to motor neurons in the spine that control muscle fibers in a particular muscle or group of muscles. For example, if someone wants to bend an elbow, motor neurons that control the biceps, brachialis, and brachioradialis muscles in the arm start firing after receiving signals from the brain. The motor neuron instructions cause these muscles to pull on the tendons and ligaments connected to the humerus, radius, and ulna bones. This pulling raises the arm at the elbow joint. The brain can then activate motor neurons connected to the triceps muscle at the back of the upper arm to straighten out the elbow.

Biomechanics experts call a group of muscle fibers and the motor neuron that controls it a motor unit. Besides initiating motion, motor units also affect muscle forces. "A motor neuron controls the amount of force that is exerted by muscle fibers,"[24] explains neuroscientist James Knierim of Johns Hopkins University. Motor neurons regulate force by generating electrical signals at a particular rate. For instance, if a motor neuron fires once, the muscle fibers it controls will twitch slightly. If it increases the rate of firing, this tells the muscle fibers to produce more force, so they twitch more. If more motor neurons start firing, this also tells muscle fibers to increase their force output.

Motor neurons also regulate muscle force output by progressively activating FT fibers, which contract faster and are larger than ST fibers. FT fibers thus exert more force than ST fibers do. When motor neurons fire slowly, ST fibers become active. As the rate of neuron firing increases, more and more FT fibers become active. These FT fibers exert greater amounts of force, but for shorter lengths of time than ST fibers can remain active.

The National Council on Strength and Fitness explains that muscles which contain more FT fibers also exert more force:

Across all contraction velocities, muscles with predominantly more type II fibers will produce more power

MOTOR NEURONS AND THE CENTRAL NERVOUS SYSTEM

Motor units consist of the muscle fiber, nerve fibers, and spinal cord cells that control a specific muscle. They initiate skeletal muscle movement and affect muscle force.

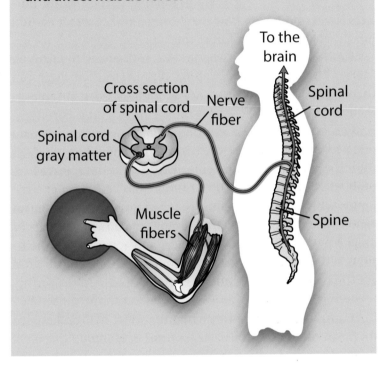

To the brain

Cross section of spinal cord

Nerve fiber

Spinal cord

Spinal cord gray matter

Muscle fibers

Spine

than muscles with predominantly type I fibers at the same velocity. This is due to certain intrinsic qualities associated with each respective fiber type. Type II fibers possess higher concentrations of ATPase [an enzyme that breaks down ATP], allowing ATP to be broken down more quickly and efficiently than type I fibers.[25]

Increasing Muscle Forces

Another factor that affects muscle force is the angular velocity at which muscles and the joints they control rotate to produce a motion like throwing a ball. Just as the motion of objects can be linear or rotational, the motion of muscles can proceed in a line or at an angle. A muscle's angular velocity increases when a joint extends and decreases when it flexes, or contracts. According to the National Council on Strength and Fitness, "Muscle power is lower at both very slow and very fast speeds. The peak power region generally occurs at approximately 40–60% of maximal angular velocity of the muscle."[26] By practicing certain skills, athletes learn to regulate how they extend and contract certain muscles to achieve the forces they desire.

The overall size of a muscle also influences the force it exerts. Muscles can exert about 0.3 newtons of force per square millimeter of area. Many athletes seek to enlarge their muscles so they can generate more force. Strength-training exercises, such as lifting weights or pushing against other types of resistance, are one method of enlarging muscles. These exercises enlarge muscles when the muscles are gradually overworked. This causes small tears in muscle fibers, which release chemicals called growth factors in response to this damage. Growth factors cause satellite cells outside muscle fibers to reproduce and to fuse with the fibers. When this happens, muscle fibers produce more actin and myosin, which add to the muscle's size.

Strength-training exercises also increase the amount of force muscles produce by changing motor neuron activity. As the book *Exercise Physiology: Basis of Human Movement in Health and Disease* explains, "as a result of a strength-training program, more muscle fibers are stimulated to contract simultaneously and muscle force increases."[27]

Strength and Power

Strength refers to the amount of force a person is capable of applying. Power, on the other hand, is the amount of force someone exerts in a given length of time. Thus, if an individual exerts a certain amount of force in a shorter span of time, he generates more power than someone who produces that amount of force over a longer time span. The force-velocity relationship is the physics equation that describes

power. It states that power equals force times distance, divided by the time elapsed. Translating this equation to biomechanics, the power exerted by a muscle "is given by the force exerted by the muscle multiplied by its shortening (or lengthening) velocity,"[28] according to the book *Biophysical Foundations of Human Movement*.

Strength and power in many muscles, from the large quadriceps muscles in the legs to smaller muscles in the wrist, hand, and fingers, are critical to bowling skills, so good bowlers seek to enhance these qualities in addition to practicing specific bowling skills. For example, strength in the fingers is important in bowling because the fingers must grip and handle a heavy ball during the arm swing. Coaches recommend increasing finger strength by pressing the fingertips of both hands together and holding the position for five to ten seconds, several times per day.

Repeatedly squeezing a soft rubber ball also increases finger strength. A study reported in 2014 by physical therapist Heather D'Errico showed that strengthening other muscles is also important for bowlers. D'Errico's study found that bowlers who participated in a program to strengthen their hip, stomach, and other core muscles showed different angular velocities in their shoulders and different hip angles that improved their ball delivery.

While strength-training exercises involve lifting weights or moving against other types of resistance, power-enhancing exercises involve lifting or manipulating light-to-medium-weight objects many times. Power-training exercises thus condition muscles to respond more quickly to signals from motor neurons. The two main types of power-training exercises are ballistics and plyometrics. In ballistics, an individual applies large amounts of force to throwing a medium-weight object like a medicine ball, with two arms, back-and-forth to another person. Ballistics increase power in the chest, shoulders, and arms. Plyometrics involves stretching a muscle group just before contracting it. This makes the muscles contract faster and more forcefully. One common plyometric exercise involves squatting (which stretches the leg and hip muscles) before jumping upwards. During the squat these muscles store potential energy like a compressed spring does. The stored energy helps the individual jump higher than he otherwise would have jumped and gradually increases the power these muscles can exert.

Other Important Qualities

Although strength and power are important in bowling, other qualities such as balance, coordination, and flexibility are also critical. This is one reason bowling is an ideal universal sport; smaller people who may lack the strength provided by huge muscles can excel at bowling by cultivating these other qualities. For example, adult male bowlers usually have more natural power and strength than female bowlers because of their larger size and weight. But as professional bowler Tammy Turner Boomershine, who was the 2009 Women's Open Champion and a member of Team USA in 2012 and 2013, states,

> While many men rely on muscle mass, we counter with attributes that are within our range of ability. I can keep up with far bigger and stronger women because of the leverage [power generated by pushing against the ground] that I consistently produce during my release. That's attributable to a combination of timing, wrist rotation, and the force that is generated by my legs.[29]

Boomershine is 5 feet 6 inches tall and weighs about 140 pounds (64kg). She explains that the power in her legs comes from lowering her center of gravity by bending her knees during the next-to-last step in the approach to the foul line. The stored energy is then released when she extends her legs.

Lowering the center of gravity also improves balance, which is critical for properly executing bowling skills. Balance involves keeping the head level when the rest of the body changes position. It also involves keeping the body weight evenly distributed over the feet. Without good balance, a bowler cannot transfer power to the ball and can also be injured by falling. Exercises that help improve balance include standing still and raising one leg at a time to the side, swinging one leg at a time back and forth, and doing squats on one leg.

Another important way in which bowlers regulate the muscle movements that contribute to bowling skills involves coordination. Coordination depends on training the brain to integrate sensory information about the position of the body, the ball, and the pins with the muscle forces needed to knock down those pins. The best way to improve coordination is to practice bowling skills over and over so the skills become automatic.

Flexibility and Bowling

Flexibility is also important in bowling. Flexibility is the ability to move muscles through their full range of motion.

Lunges or squats are among the stretches recommended for bowlers to increase and maintain flexibility in the legs and hips.

It can be increased by stretching the muscles. Since warm muscles stretch more easily than cold muscles do, sports doctors recommend warming up the muscles by walking a short distance or doing other simple exercises before stretching to improve flexibility.

Increasing the flexibility of muscles throughout the body can improve bowling skills. One area that is especially important is the legs and hips, since these body parts play a big role in generating power that can be transferred to the ball. Bowling coaches recommend exercises such as touching the toes and doing lunges and squats to stretch the legs and hips. They also recommend paying particular attention to stretching the hand and wrist of the throwing arm by rolling them back and forth and flexing them up and down. It is also important to stretch the shoulders by reaching the arms across the chest or behind the back, since the shoulders play a big role in the arm swing. Stretching muscles before bowling helps performance, in part because the more a muscle stretches and contracts, the more force it produces. Flexible, stretched-out muscles are also less likely to be strained or torn.

Clothing and Flexibility

Bowling well requires muscle flexibility and the ability to move body parts freely. Bowlers recognized the importance of these factors long before people—especially women—began wearing comfortable clothing while bowling. For example, an 1887 article in the *St. Paul Daily Globe* newspaper discussed how bowling alley proprietors complained about the tight corsets that ladies wore during this era to make their waists appear tiny. The reason they complained was that corsets prevented women from bending enough to launch a bowling ball close to the lane. Dropping the ball from high up, known as lofting the ball, can damage the lanes because objects dropped from higher up accelerate more and therefore hit the ground with more force, according to Newton's second law of motion. The article stated:

> Proprietors of alleys sometimes object to letting ladies play because they are apt to loft the balls and injure the alleys. When they play without corsets, however, and can bend over enough to roll a ball instead of dropping it from the height of the knee, no objections are made. . . . Good bowling requires perfect freedom of action, and women who play in rational attire soon find that the exercise strengthens them and renders corsets unnecessary.

St. Paul Daily Globe. "Ladies Who Practice Bowling Do Not Generally Feel the Need of Corsets." January 23, 1887, http://chroniclingamerica.loc.gov/lccn/sn 90059522/1887-01-23/ed-1/seq-18/.

Although bowling skills rely on short expenditures of muscle energy that rely more on power, balance, and flexibility rather than on cardiovascular fitness and aerobic energy, coaches still recommend that bowlers improve their cardiovascular fitness with exercises such as brisk walking or jogging. This is because cardiovascular fitness is important for reducing fatigue during long bowling sessions and for recovering quickly after tournaments.

Conditioning the body and practicing bowling skills to allow for optimal performance are only part of what makes a good bowler, however. Mental qualities such as concentration, motivation, and persistence are equally important in determining how well a bowler plays the game.

CHAPTER 4

The Mental Game

Bowling coaches and sports psychologists say the mental aspects of bowling are as important as the physical ones in determining how well an individual bowls. As professional bowling champion and coach Michelle Mullen writes in her book *Bowling Fundamentals*, "Developing a strong mental game will help you become a good bowler, whereas a great mental game will help you become a great bowler. The better your physical game is, the more important your mental game becomes to your success."[30]

Sports psychology is a sub-field of psychology that helps athletes develop mental and emotional skills that allow them to do their best and to perform consistently. Psychologist Norman Triplett published the first studies on the social and psychological factors that impact sports performance in 1898. His studies demonstrated that athletes perform better in bicycle races when they have a competitor. This helped mental health experts realize that the psyche (mind) plays a big role in sports. The first sports psychology laboratory opened in Germany in 1920; after this the field of sports psychology developed rapidly. Modern sports psychologists use a variety of behavioral and talking therapies to help all types of athletes develop positive mental skills that enhance their physical skills. Coaches also incorporate these techniques into their teaching and training programs.

Cara Honeychurch and Mental Weapons

Professional bowler Cara Honeychurch was the Women's Bowling Association's Rookie of the Year in 2000 and has received many other awards and honors. She wrote about one incident in the 1998 Commonwealth Games in Malaysia that illustrates the importance of believing in oneself and being able to concentrate. These qualities allowed her to overcome adverse conditions and win medals in this competition.

The Malaysian bowling team believed that Honeychurch was the biggest threat to their quest to win the games. So they distracted her in hopes that she would not bowl well. They even gave their plan a name: Operation Cara. As part of this campaign, local media published unfavorable stories about Honeychurch. Malaysian team members and spectators blew horns and made other loud noises while Honeychurch bowled. She later wrote, "As you can imagine, it took a great deal of concentration and belief in myself to overcome such trying circumstances. However, I was able to do so, and this resulted in my winning three gold medals."

Quoted in John Jowdy. *Bowling Execution.* Champaign, IL: Human Kinetics, 2009, p. 6.

In discussing the importance of teaching strong mental skills along with physical skills, sports psychologist Dean Hinitz states in his book *Focused for Bowling,* "Having a strong mental game means being able to call forth your best qualities when you need them—in the heart of competition, for example. It is like having a warrior within you to assist you whenever necessary."[31]

Positive Thinking

Positive thinking is one concept coaches and sports psychologists emphasize as being important in fostering mental toughness. Many teach techniques such as positive self-talk to help bowlers reach their potential, since studies have shown that people learn to believe what they say and think. For example, former Team USA member and Wichita State University bowling coach Gordon Vadakin attributes much of his team's success to his requirement that bowlers repeat

Athletes who develop their ability to engage positive thoughts and attitudes also improve their performance.

positive phrases such as "I always make great shots"[32] several times per day.

Indeed, many coaches and sports psychologists point out that giving oneself or others negative instructions that include the words "not" or "no" is much less likely to lead to improvements than positive corrections are. For instance, rather than saying "do not grip the ball so tightly," it is more productive to say "I can improve my shot by relaxing my arm and hand." In a similar manner, having a negative attitude about new challenges, such as new and different oil patterns on the lane, can lead bowlers to balk at trying a new starting place behind the foul line or trying a different ball when appropriate. On the other hand, a positive attitude that emphasizes doing whatever needs to be done to adapt to new conditions is more likely to result in improvements.

An important consequence of positive thinking is that it helps improve self-confidence, which is essential for bowling well. People who believe they can do something well are much more likely to do so than those who lack this confidence. However, although many experts believe self-confidence grows out of winning, Hinitz is one psychologist who believes this is not necessarily true. He writes, "Many people believe that confidence comes from good results. In reality, confidence is born out of learning to trust oneself; it comes from knowing that you will bring all your skill and training to bear under any circumstance."[33] Confidence is thus closely tied to another important mental quality—motivation—since athletes who are motivated are willing to do whatever it takes to achieve their goals.

Motivation

Motivation is closely tied to positive thinking as well as to self-confidence, and although each of these qualities feeds the others, in most cases motivation precedes the others. Bowlers who are not motivated to improve can repeat all the positive thoughts in the world without results because being motivated is what actually leads them to act on these thoughts. Motivation can be internal or external. Much of an individual's motivation to learn and succeed comes from inside, and different people are motivated by different internal factors. For some, the desire to improve in order to have fun with family or friends is sufficient motivation to take bowling lessons and practice diligently. For others, the desire to win championships is a primary motivating factor. External motivations are derived from others, such as the desire to please a parent or group of friends or to receive praise and notoriety from the public. Good coaches can also be powerful motivating forces for athletes, especially those coaches with contagious positive attitudes who build up athletes' self-confidence along with their skills.

Although external motivators play a role, sports psychologist JoAnn Dahlkoetter writes that internal motivation is especially important in competitive success: "To truly excel as an athlete you must have an inner fire, that drive, simply to become the best you can be. . . . Motivation is energy, and that sense of self-directedness is one of the most powerful sources of energy available to an athlete."[34] However, Dahlkoetter emphasizes that motivation and drive are not necessarily inborn and can be learned. One method she uses to enhance motivation is positive self-talk, which also helps athletes translate motivation into improved athletic skills. This, in turn, involves another important mental quality called motor learning.

Motor Learning

Motor learning involves training the nervous system and muscles to work in harmony to execute the complex motions that constitute sports skills. As an individual practices these skills, the brain learns to automatically instruct the muscles and other body parts to execute the skills correctly, so the athlete does not have to think about coordinating each component. Coaches help with the motor learning process by offering feedback. For instance, a coach may tell a bowler that her backswing will improve if she pulls her

With repeated practice, a bowler can improve her motor learning so that her muscles act automatically without thinking.

arm back at a forty-five degree angle. This type of feedback is known as external feedback. The bowler can turn this external feedback into internal feedback by practicing the movement repeatedly. Eventually, the muscles and other body parts provide internal feedback to the brain to let it know that they are positioned correctly. The brain then goes to the next step in the motor learning sequence.

However, when a bowler does not learn bowling skills correctly or learns skills that do not suit his abilities, undoing this motor learning and learning new movement patterns can be difficult. Coaches recognize this, and part of their job involves motivating bowlers to accept the need to do things differently if they want to improve. Michelle Mullen, for example, writes that "To improve as a bowler, you need to be willing to get out of, and expand, your comfort zones. Whether you are learning to play a different arrow on the lane or adjusting to a different feel with your timing, you need to get out of your current comfort zone to become a better bowler."[35]

Motivation and positive self-talk both play a big role in influencing how quickly and how well motor learning of new skills occurs. Those who are motivated to improve take the time to keep practicing, and thus tend to learn faster and better. Those who practice positive mental exercises such as imagery also experience faster motor learning.

Imagery

Many coaches and sports psychologists recommend imagery, or visualization, to help athletes learn new or better skills or to bolster their confidence. Imagery involves an athlete imagining himself performing certain skills correctly, using one or more sensory images. In his book *Winning Bowling*, 1970s bowling champion Earl Anthony discusses the link between positive thinking and imagery:

> By imprinting your imagination in advance you have that desirable positive thought which may block out another undesirable one, a thought or fear that you might not make the shot that confronts you. Remember that the mind can only have one thought at a time, and your goal is to emphasize the positive thoughts so as to exclude negative ones.[36]

Dahlkoetter is one sports psychologist who advises her clients to incorporate as many senses as possible into their imagery sessions; she recommends that they imagine what a particular motion looks like, feels like, and even sounds like. All types of imagery have been proven to hasten motor learning and to help athletes execute skills consistently. Thus, this type of mental "workout" guides the body's actions, illustrating the extent to which mental and physical actions are intertwined. As psychologist Jim Taylor explains in a *Psychology Today* article, "Imagery is used by virtually all great athletes and research has shown that, when combined with actual practice, [it] improves performance more than practice alone. Imagery also isn't just a mental experience that occurs in your head, but rather impacts you in every way: psychologically, emotionally, physically, technically, and tactically."[37]

Many athletes employ imagery during practice sessions as well as during competitions; sometimes as often as before beginning each bowling shot. Dahlkoetter explains that "using imagery or visualization you can create, in vivid

How Imagery Works

An important study in the early 1990s by researchers at the University of Parma in Italy provided the first clues about how and why imagery helps athletes learn skills. While studying brain activity in rhesus monkeys, the researchers accidently discovered that the monkeys' brains showed identical activity when viewing certain actions and when actually performing those actions. For instance, a researcher picked up a banana while a monkey watched. This created activity in the same area of the monkey's brain that became active when the monkey itself picked up a banana. Thus, the monkey's brain acted like it had performed an action when it merely viewed someone else performing the action. The researchers called the neurons that responded in this manner mirror neurons.

Subsequent research in 2004 by neuroscientist Daniel Glaser and his colleagues at University College London used magnetic resonance imaging (MRI) to compare brain activity in capoeira dancers and Royal Ballet dancers to brain activity in non-dancers. (Capoeira is a Brazilian martial art dance style.) The scientists showed participants videos of ballet and capoeira movements. They found that ballet dancers showed activity in the premotor cortex area of the brain while viewing ballet moves. Capoeira dancers showed activity in this area while viewing capoeira moves. The premotor cortex controls muscle movements. The dancers' brains thus behaved as though they were actually performing familiar movements when they viewed others performing those movements. Athletes now use these principles to enhance motor learning by imagining themselves performing certain actions.

detail, a replay of one of your best performances in the past, or you can mentally rehearse an upcoming event, and you can learn to see yourself doing it right."[38] Studies also indicate that imagery can greatly enhance the important mental quality of concentration, or focus.

The Importance of Focus

One of the most important mental qualities for bowlers who seek to improve their skills and to perform well is the ability to stay focused. Indeed, coaches and trainers emphasize that one of the most efficient ways of mastering new skills is to focus on one motion at a time before putting these motions together into an integrated whole. For instance, when a bowler is working on improving the timing in his approach to the foul line, coaches recommend focusing on correcting and mastering each part of the arm motions, followed by mastering each part of the leg motions, before putting the arm and leg motions together.

A strong focus while bowling includes not letting other people distract one from concentrating on the immediate task at hand. In his book *Bowling Execution*, renowned bowling coach John Jowdy writes that the ability to concentrate and tune out distractions can override deficiencies in technique and often makes the difference between good and great bowlers. For example, according to Jowdy, professional bowler Don Johnson "admitted that he was far less talented than most of his competitors, yet he managed to win 26 PBA titles before injuries forced him into retirement. His focus was so intense that he was oblivious to sounds and other distractions that would have rattled average bowlers, especially in critical situations. His ability to manage distractions led to his success."[39]

Experts also emphasize the importance of focusing on the present. This includes not focusing on beating someone else, on winning a tournament, or on regretting a missed shot because these distractions put one's focus on the past or future rather than on the present. As Vadakin states in a *Bowling This Month* article,

> No bowler has a crystal ball to predict the future, but they do have the ability to vividly stay present and make one clear and focused shot at a time. Emotions like fear, dread, and anxiety are examples of future thinking. Thoughts or feelings like anger and frustration are usually examples of past thinking. Reliving past failures such as "I always mess up in close matches," is practicing being in the past. Whatever you practice, you get good at.[40]

KINGPIN

95%

The component of the game that is mental for elite competitive bowlers, according to sports psychologists; the other 5 percent is physical

Wes Malott displays the focus that helped him win his first career title in 2005. Tuning out distractions and staying focused on the present help an athlete avoid mistakes.

Failing to focus on the present often leads to mistakes in tactics and technique. "When I lose my balance, it is almost always because my mind wandered and I lost focus,"[41] Mullen explains. Many times, these types of mistakes come from focusing on the wrong priorities in addition to letting one's mind wander. One of the most common culprits is concentrating on how important the next shot is to winning a tournament rather than simply focusing on immediate concerns like lane conditions, the arm swing, and the legwork. "If you feel pressure to make something happen, you can put yourself in bowler's jail. Over-attention to results creates fear based bowling. When this happens, you are trying not to make bad shots and bowl badly instead of trying to make good shots and bowl well,"[42] states Hinitz in a *Bowling This Month* article.

Different bowlers use different methods of enhancing their focusing abilities. For instance, Earl Anthony writes that he tuned out external distractions by purposefully directing his attention to one object at a time, such as a lane arrow, the lane oil pattern, or the ball: "My concentration on a certain target, such as one of the lane marker arrows is like having a powerful searchlight aimed at it, a searchlight which I control and with determination can keep in control until I release it once the assigned task, hitting the target, is completed."[43]

High-Pressure Situations

The ability to focus can also impact another important mental quality for bowlers—the ability to remain calm and relaxed under high-pressure situations, such as during a close competition with big money stakes for a professional bowler. For recreational bowlers, remaining calm is also important; in such cases, pressure may come from simply wanting to improve one's score or from not wanting to disappoint one's team in a bowling league. One reason remaining calm is so important in bowling is that mental tension tightens muscles throughout the body, and a proper arm swing and legwork depend on relaxed muscles.

Sports psychologists say some people have a natural ability to remain calm under pressure, while others tense up or even throw tantrums if they are stressed or miss a shot. However, the ability to remain calm can be practiced and learned. As former professional bowler Robert Strickland and communications professor William Powers write in their book *Bowling Tough*, "Tough bowlers are not immune to stress. They just deal with it effectively. Because they know that anxiety or stress is a natural part of high-level

The Power of Determination

Some bowlers have natural physical attributes that help them become champions. Don Johnson, however, who was named one of the twenty best bowlers of the century in 2001, succeeded because of determination. Johnson watched his first bowling match on television at age thirteen. The match featured George Howard and Dick Weber, who were both small and thin. Johnson, who loved sports but was not big enough to play football or basketball, stated in a Bowling News USA article, "I was a little, skinny runt kid, and I thought, 'Man, this is the sport for me!' I decided that bowling was what I was going to do in life." He began bowling, and after high school got a job at a local bowling center, where he bowled about twenty games a day to try to improve. It still took him many years to improve to the point that he could join the PBA. At age eighteen, he was still averaging scores of about 165. However, as the article states, "What Johnson lacked in ability, he made up for in determination." In 1962, at age twenty-two, he finally qualified for the PBA, and in 1964 he began winning tournaments. He continued to improve by bowling in 260 consecutive tournaments between 1963 and 1970. He won 26 PBA titles before retiring from competition because of a thumb injury in 1980. Johnson taught hundreds of students, many of whom became champions, for another eighteen years.

Quoted in Paul Kreins. "The Kokomo Kid." *Bowling News USA*, May 5, 2003. www.stormbowling.com/news/2003/05/927.

competition, they simply meet it head-on and control their reactions to it."[44]

One bowler known for effectively meeting stress head-on is professional bowler Johnny Petraglia. In an interview posted on the Action Bowlers website, Petraglia was asked if his legs shake when he is in a pressure situation. Petraglia replied, "Yes I shake. But I've learned that that's where all the fun is. The way to combat it is to take the pressure and put it in front of you. Now if I need a strike to win a match, I say things like my heart is beating faster, my palms are sweaty, I know 10 million people are watching me and I'm good enough to handle it. As long as the last thought is positive you have a great chance for success."[45]

Different techniques for enhancing the ability to remain calm under stress work best for different people, but most involve some form of positive thinking. For example, professional bowler Mike Aulby, known for winning numerous important tournaments during the 1980s and 1990s, bowled poorly in 1994. That year, his father passed away and he was stressed out from his responsibilities as PBA president. Aulby consulted sports psychiatrist Eva Burridge, and in 1995 he again won the Tournament of Champions. He told the *Los Angeles Times* that "[Burridge] has helped me with the pressure situations and helped with mental self-talk to stay focused."[46] Another method of coping with pressure involves visualization. By mentally reviewing how a previous successful shot in a stressful situation looked and felt, bowlers can often overcome their jitters in present stressful conditions. In fact, many good bowlers take a few seconds to visualize how a perfect execution looks before each shot.

Burnout and Bowling

No matter how well bowlers tackle pressure situations, many suffer the performance slumps and burnouts that affect many athletes, especially after months or years of intense training and competition. According to Hinitz, "Burnout is the hidden undertow of the serious athlete. It sneaks up on the bowler, sucking energy, excitement, and enthusiasm, and subtly drowning competitive spirit."[47] Psychologists find that burnout is most likely to affect the hardest workers and the highest achievers, particularly those who do not take frequent breaks from training or competition. Those who are most motivated to win, who demand perfection from themselves, and who mentally punish themselves for mistakes are also at high risk for burnout.

When competitive bowlers burn out or experience performance slumps, they often become very frustrated about

Bowling can be a high pressure sport, and players who punish themselves mentally for mistakes have a higher risk for burnout.

their sub-standard performance. Some continue to compete until poor performance forces them to stop. Some quit permanently, while others simply take a break to rest or to seek help from a coach or sports psychologist. However, it often takes a while for a bowler to recognize burnout because it tends to develop gradually. Some bowlers believe their lack of enthusiasm and feelings of being emotionally overwhelmed are simply instances of temporary disappointment over losing a match or tournament. But soon they or others around them realize that the problem is much more serious.

Sports psychologists say that taking an extended break from competition is often a good method of dealing with burnout, as long as the break includes working on changing one's unproductive mental habits such as mental self-punishment. Working with a new coach or psychologist can help athletes work on self-acceptance, positive thinking, and other productive attributes. As Powers and Strickland write, "Tough bowlers are aware of the times when they failed—but only for a short time. They simply 'go back to the drawing board' and work out a winning strategy."[48]

Just as successful bowlers constantly strive to improve their physical game, they also recognize that these physical skills are intricately tied to mental processes. They thus take time to improve their mental strengths as well. Each time they stand ready to execute a shot, both their physical and mental skills unite to make the shot as effective as possible.

CHAPTER 5

Pre-Throw Strategies

O ne of the most important skills that a bowler's mental and physical preparation and training contribute to is consistency. As Mike Aulby, professional bowler Dave Ferraro, and sports writer Dan Herbst explain in their book *Bowling 200+: Winning Strategies to Up Your Average and Improve Your Game,* "Good bowling involves repetition. The first-rate player can duplicate the same series of motions time after time to produce consistent shot making."[49] But before a bowler can apply his physical training and psychological weapons to generate effective and consistent skills, he needs the right equipment, must understand the ideal methods of achieving strikes and spares, and must master a consistent pre-throw routine that leads into a fluid approach and ball delivery.

The Right Ball

Using the right ball is critical for bowling skills and consistency, so competitive bowlers generally use custom-made balls. The qualities of these balls depend on the bowler's physical attributes and bowling style and on lane conditions. For example, while most competitive bowlers usually use reactive resin balls, many switch to a plastic ball when shooting spares if the position of the remaining pins makes

Choosing the proper ball is crucial in bowling. Among the most important considerations are the ball's weight and how it fits the bowler's hand and fingers.

it important not to make the ball hook. This is especially true when only one pin remains, and the bowler wishes to aim straight for that pin. Unlike reactive resin balls, plastic balls have little friction with the lane and roll in a straight line.

Bowling balls range from 6 to 16 pounds (3 to 7kg). The ideal ball weight for a particular bowler is one that allows him to perform a consistent arm swing without straining to lift and control the ball. With older bowling balls, the hitting power depended mostly on the weight (because of Newton's second law), so many bowlers tried to use the heaviest possible ball. Today, however, stronger ball cores impart more power. As Mullen explains, "Bowling balls today hit harder, even in lighter weights. For this reason, many of the male professional bowlers do not throw 16 pounds [7kg]. If you have to labor to push the ball out into the swing or cannot let the ball swing fully into the backswing, or if your ball speed is too slow, consider using a lighter ball."[50]

Besides using a ball with the correct weight, many bowlers purchase balls with custom-drilled holes. Most balls have three holes—two finger holes and one thumbhole. Some bowlers choose to have a fourth hole called a pinkie hole drilled to help them grip the ball more easily. The size, span, and pitch of each hole is important. The hole size should allow the fingers and thumb to fit in all the way, without fitting too snugly or too loosely. If the holes are too large, this forces the bowler to grip the ball too tightly and does not allow a relaxed arm swing or fluid ball release. If they are too small, this can be uncomfortable, can scrape the fingers, and can interfere with the ball release.

The span is the distance from the finger holes to the thumbhole. Ball designers measure the bowler's hand to determine the correct span, which allows the fingers and thumb to fit inside comfortably. If the span is too long or too short, the fingers will not fit into the holes properly. This will disrupt the ability to rotate the rest of the hand to add spin and hook to the ball when the fingers leave the holes.

The pitch is the angle at which the holes are drilled. A hole drilled toward the ball's center has a zero, or no angle, pitch. One that is drilled at an angle toward the palm of the hand has a forward pitch, which helps bowlers hold onto the ball. A hole drilled at an angle away from the palm has a reverse pitch, which helps bowlers release the ball sooner and more easily. The proper pitch depends on the span between an individual's fingers and thumb and on his finger flexibility. Those with a shorter span usually need holes with a forward pitch. Those with a longer span need a reverse pitch, but too much reverse pitch will force a bowler to hold onto the ball too long because he will have to squeeze it tightly during the backswing so as not to drop it.

Get a Grip

The way in which a bowler grips the ball also influences the ideal pitch and span. Different bowlers use different grips. Most beginners use a conventional grip, where the fingers and thumb go all the way into the holes up to the second joint. Most elite bowlers use a fingertip grip, where the fingers only go into the holes up to the first joint. This grip allows the bowler to put more spin on the ball because the fingers quickly follow the thumb in exiting the holes. The ball then rolls off the fingers in a way that adds spin. Those who use a fingertip grip often need more reverse pitch in the finger holes to allow the finger pads to stay flush against the front of the holes for comfort and the best ball release. Those who use a fingertip grip also need a greater span between the holes.

Most bowlers who use a fingertip grip choose to have rubber finger inserts called finger grips glued into the finger holes. Many also use a removable thumb insert called a slug. Some also put bowler's tape into the thumbhole when the

The ideal pitch and span of the finger holes depend on the bowler's preferred grip style.

thumb is its normal size and remove the tape if the thumb swells during a game, which often happens.

Ideal Bowling Shots

The reason having the right ball and grip are so important is that these factors give bowlers the best chance of making an ideal shot. For example, most competitive bowlers use reactive resin balls, at least on their first shot, because a ball that hooks and hits the pins at an angle is most likely to result in a strike. Bowlers refer to the exact location at which they aim to place the ball as the pocket. Hitting the pocket involves hitting a 1-inch-wide (2.5cm) target 60 feet (18m) away from the foul line. For a right-handed bowler, this means the ball ideally enters what is called the 1-3 pocket, between the 1-pin and the 3-pin. For a left-handed bowler, the ball enters the 1-2 pocket.

Hitting a perfect bowling shot depends in large part on using the proper ball and grip.

The angle at which the ball enters the pocket is extremely important. As USBC technical director Neil Stremmel explains, the angle "plays an enormous role in strike

HITTING THE POCKET

For right-handed bowlers, hitting the pocket between pins 1 and 3 produces the ideal shot. (The trajectory for left-handed bowlers is a mirror image, aiming instead for the pocket between pins 1 and 2.) The bowling ball's direct hit topples pins 1, 3, 5, and 9, while the remaining pins are knocked down like dominoes by these four pins.

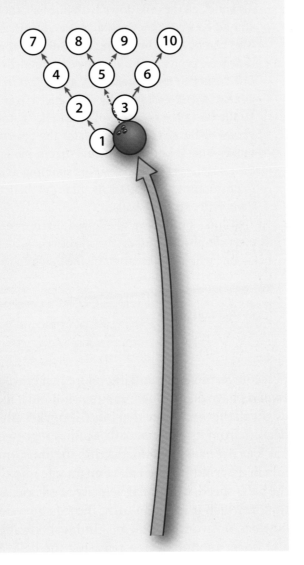

Bowling Strikes Circa 1887

Knowledge about ideal methods of hitting bowling pins has improved with modern technologies that measure ball speed, rotation, and pocket angles. However, bowlers understood much about these methods long before these technologies were invented. For example, a January 23, 1887 article in the *St. Paul Daily Globe* stated:

> To knock all the pins down with one ball, the head pin should be struck on the side with considerable force. This can be done by rolling the ball in a straight line down the center of the alley, by straight delivery from one corner to the center, or by a ball sent in a curved course. The cross ball is the most effective and is used by the best players. Some of them play a straight ball very well, but if it happens to catch the head pin full, it makes what is known as a "gut," that is, ploughs a lane through the set and leaves pins standing at each side in positions that make it difficult to get them all down, even with two more balls.

At that time, bowlers were allowed three shots per frame. The article also discussed the effectiveness of the "skew" ball—one with spin imparted by the bowler's wrist.

Minnesota Historical Society. "Bowling and Rackets." *St. Paul Daily Globe*, January 23, 1887. http://chroniclingamerica.loc.gov/lccn/sn90059522/1887-01 -23/ed-1/seq-18.pdf.

percentage, pin carry and, therefore in a bowler's average."[51] Experts have determined that the shot most likely to knock down all the pins is one that hits the pocket after curving six degrees from its original path. Studies reported in the journal *Sports Engineering* found that the most important factors in determining the ball's entry angle into the pocket are the ball's speed, its angular velocity at release, and the direction in which it spins. In turn, these factors depend on the bowler's footwork, arm swing, timing, body angle, and wrist and finger motions when releasing the ball. According to

Stremmel, "A ball thrown with 350 rpm at about 18 miles per hour [29 kmh] appears to be the optimum rev rate. . . . [P]reliminary research shows that at this rate a bowling ball seems to skid the proper amount to achieve optimum entry angle."[52]

During an ideal shot, the ball only touches four pins. For a right-handed bowler, the ball first hits the 1-pin and the 3-pin. The 1-pin then hits the 2-pin, which hits the 4-pin, which hits the 7-pin. The 3-pin hits the 6-pin, which hits the 10-pin. After hitting the 1-pin and the 3-pin, the ball ideally hits the 5-pin, pushing the 5-pin into the 8-pin. The ball then hits the 9-pin. For a left-handed bowler, the ideal shot involves the ball hitting the 1-pin and the 2-pin, then the 5-pin, then the 8-pin. The 1-pin hits the 3-pin, which hits the 6-pin, which hits the 10-pin. The 2-pin hits the 4-pin, which hits the 7-pin. The 5-pin topples the 9-pin. Bowling experts state that the 5-pin, known as the kingpin, is the most critical pin in the chain reaction. Earl Anthony explains in *Winning Bowling*, "Miss it with your ball or fail to get it with pin action that causes another pin to knock it down and you do not have a strike."[53]

The ideal shot, however, often does not happen. The ball may head sideways after hitting the headpin (the 1-pin) if it hits the pocket at the wrong angle. Sometimes the ball or pins lack the momentum to knock down all the pins. If the ball has too much power, a pocket hit may not result in a strike if the ball keeps hooking and hits the center of the 5-pin instead of the side, in which case the 5-pin will not hit the 8-pin or the 9-pin. On the other hand, failing to hit the pocket can result in a strike if the ball has enough power and spin to make the headpin bounce off the side wall and knock over the 10-pin. This is why most elite bowlers favor shooting hook shots that pack more power; a strike can occur even with errors in accuracy. When a bowler throws a straight ball that does not hook, it must hit the pocket exactly right to achieve a strike.

KINGPIN

1,023

The number of different possible spare combinations of pins left after the first roll in bowling.

Shooting Spares

When a bowler fails to make a strike, any of the pins can be left standing. Observing which pins are left and formulating the best spare-shooting strategy is extremely important in such cases. Oftentimes, this strategy includes changing bowling balls or not adding spin and hook to the ball, particularly if aiming at a single pin. According to the USBC, "The key to single pin spares is to be accurate. A straight ball is more accurate than a curve release. If you use a big curve, get a plastic ball and/or learn to release the ball straight."[54] Coaches also recommend that bowlers face the pin at which they are aiming and maintain that position while walking to the foul line.

A bowler may also need to change his starting position and the angle at which he shoots a spare shot. For example, if the four-pin is left standing, a right-handed bowler will probably move several boards to the right of where he stood on his first shot. When two or more pins remain, a bowler ideally aims to throw the ball so its momentum and the pins' momentum knock down all the remaining pins. However, when there is a gap between two or more remaining pins (known as a split), it is often difficult to hit all of them. Anthony explains that this can be done "by striking the pin in the front line thinly, that is, just barely touching it with your ball, and forcing it to fly across the lane at an oblique angle and thus take out the remaining pin or pins."[55] Another difficult situation occurs when the pins that remain are the ten-pin and/or the seven-pin, located in the back corners, closest to the gutters. Coaches say it is virtually impossible to hit both and is often difficult to hit even one of these pins. Shooting from the left side of the foul line to hit a pin on the right side of the lane gives bowlers the best chance of hitting a corner pin.

Assessing Lane Conditions

Evaluating the best way of hitting the pocket on the first throw or shooting a spare on the second includes carefully focusing on and assessing lane conditions. While the

amount and patterns of lane oil differ among bowling centers, professional bowlers face even more challenging oil conditions because professional tournaments use complex oil patterns known as challenge patterns to test competitors' ability to adapt to new conditions. These challenge patterns have names like Chameleon, Cheetah, Scorpion, Shark, and Viper. The Cheetah pattern, for example, is 35 feet (11m) long, with the heaviest oil in the center of the lane's first 10 feet (3m), and with progressively less oil further out. This pattern forces bowlers to throw the ball so it rolls close to the gutters. With any oil pattern, both mental and physical skills are critical in determining a shot's effectiveness.

Figuring out oil patterns is difficult because the oil is invisible. Sometimes players are told that the oil pattern is a typical house shot pattern, with more oil in the middle of the lane and less at the sides, or a challenge pattern, which may involve many different configurations. But usually elite players are not informed about oil patterns; indeed, Jowdy writes that "seeking a line to the pocket is like running an

Detecting the oil pattern used on a bowling lane is extremely difficult because the oil is invisible.

Challenge Oil Patterns

Professional bowling tournaments use challenge oil patterns to force competitors to adapt their bowling style to different lane conditions.

- The Chameleon is 39 feet (11.9m) long and includes oil placed in strips on the lane. This requires players to roll the ball in a specific zone.
- The Cheetah is 35 feet (10.7m) long and places the heaviest oil in the lane's central portion of the first 10 feet (3m), with progressively less oil further out in the center. It pushes bowlers to roll the ball close to the gutters.
- The Scorpion is 41 feet (12.5m) long and places oil in strips similar to those in the Chameleon, but with thicker oil extending further out. This makes it difficult to get the ball to hook enough before striking the pins.
- The Shark is 44 feet (13.4m) long and places the most oil close to the gutters until just over 30 feet (9.1m) out, when the most oil is around the lane's center for about 14 more feet (4m). Bowlers tend to send the ball down the lane's center with this pattern.
- The Viper is 37 feet (11.3m) long. It places the most oil in the lane's center until 10 feet (3m) out, then concentrates oil next to the gutters until 30 feet (9.1m) out, when the oil extends the full width of the lane up to the pins. This pattern allows bowlers to use a variety of strategies.

obstacle course while blindfolded."[56] Bowlers must discover an oil pattern by observing how the ball acts during their practice shots. Experts call this "reading" the lanes. Then, bowlers make educated guesses to determine their strategy. Oil patterns also change as a game progresses, since bowling balls smear and absorb some of the oil, so the lane-reading process must be constantly repeated.

Learning to read the lanes effectively and to make the proper changes in position and strategy take much practice and experience, and adjusting to new oil patterns can be challenging even for experienced bowlers. For example, professional bowler Michael Haugen Jr. described his experience at a 2013 PBA tournament:

> This week, the PBA made changes to the patterns we use and I became extremely confused. My ball was hooking in places it didn't before. . . . There was also a change to the type of oil we use. This oil seemed to get down the lane faster than the previous oil, so more changes to learn and deal with. I struggled the first 2 days, made some positive changes and bowled better the 3rd and 4th day.[57]

Boards and Breakpoints

The types of changes bowlers make in response to changing lane conditions include changing their starting point and re-calculating the ball's breakpoint. For instance, coaches say that if a right-handed player is missing the pocket, with the ball going to the right of the pocket, he should move his feet to the right at the foul line. This changes the angle at which the ball hits the pocket. When moving the starting position, bowlers usually count boards, arrows, or dots. Each lane has thirty-nine boards and seven arrows. Seven dots on the foul line are lined up with the seven arrows. Coaches advise shifting one's position a certain number of boards or dots to change the ball's angle a certain amount, based on a particular bowler's style.

Another important aspect of adjusting to lane conditions involves judging how far out on the lane to project the ball so it curves properly to hit the pocket. The projection point is called the breakpoint. This is the point at which the ball starts to hook after proceeding straight down the lane. A player needs to know how far out the oil pattern extends to calculate the breakpoint. The further out the oil extends, the closer to the pocket the breakpoint will be. Since the lane

Bowlers can adjust the angle at which the ball hits the pins by changing where they move their feet in relation to the dots on the foul line.

is 60 feet (18m) long and the pocket is on board number seventeen-and-a-half, bowling experts developed an equation called the rule of thirty-one to help with determining the breakpoint. The breakpoint lies at the board whose number equals the length of the oil pattern, minus thirty-one. Thus, if a lane is oiled for 42 feet (13m), the breakpoint is around the eleventh board, which is about 42 feet (13m) down the lane. Bowlers aim to put enough speed and spin on the ball so it will hook at the breakpoint and will thus have the best chance of hitting the pocket.

Good bowlers learn to judge the oil volume, as well as its pattern, by observing how much the ball skids before it hooks. The oil volume affects the type of ball it is best to use. If a lane has heavy oil volume, it is best to use a ball with a rougher, or lower-grit, cover to give it more friction so it will not slide into the pins before hooking. A light oil volume calls for a smoother ball, with a higher grit. Reactive resin ball covers are rated by their grit, or roughness. Bowlers can also alter a ball's surface by sanding it with abrasive pads.

The Pre-Throw Routine

Besides choosing the best ball for the shot, choosing the ideal starting place, and determining how much spin and hook the shot needs, most good bowlers include a series of physical motions in their individual pre-throw routines. These motions often include wiping oil off the ball, wiping off the bottom of the shoes so they don't slip, and checking on the tape in the ball holes. Aulby explains, "Prior to beginning my delivery I go through precisely the same series of motions every time. This isn't superstition. Rather, it's a group of preparatory activities that put me in the best stead to make a good shot. I want to be physically and mentally set *before* I take that initial step."[58]

CHAPTER 6

Coordinating Physics and Biomechanics

O nce a bowler determines the best strategy for beginning a throw and completes the pre-throw routine,
executing the throw with the proper footwork and
arm swing techniques involves coordinating the physics
and biomechanics of moving the body and transferring the
ideal amount of force, rotation, and revolution to the ball.
The bowler's stance upon beginning the approach to the
foul line is one critical factor in determining the outcome
of the throw. As Mullen writes, "The starting position, or
stance, sets the tone for the motion that follows. . . . Starting
in a sound, leveraged position with a relaxed body will help
you develop a good approach."[59]

In a proper stance, the bowler stands with her feet close
together and knees slightly bent. The spine is slightly tilted
forward, with the body's center of gravity over the legs. The
feet, hips, and shoulders should face the target. A right-
handed bowler's right foot should be slightly behind the left
foot, with more weight on the left foot so the right foot is
free to begin moving. This positions the body so the person
will end up on the correct foot for releasing the ball. When
the ball is released, a right-handed player should end up on
her left foot, with her right leg behind the body.

The ball should be supported with both hands, but most
of its weight should be on the non-dominant hand. This

helps the swing arm (the right arm in a right-handed person) relax during the backswing. Before the arm swing begins, both elbows are flexed, and the swing arm's elbow should be next to the ribs. The ball should be held in line with the inside of the right shoulder for a right-handed bowler, close to the body.

Before the arm swing begins, the ball should be supported with both hands with most of the weight on the bowler's non-dominant hand.

The Approach

Once in a proper stance, the bowler steps into the approach to the foul line. Here, the goal is to synchronize the arm swing and footwork, both of which are critical in the proper ball release, while keeping the body facing the target and keeping one's eyes on the target. As record-breaking amateur bowler Darin Baginski states in the book *Bowler's Handbook*, watching the target while coordinating the other elements of the approach can be difficult, but is essential: "If I take my eye off the target before I release the ball I will throw a bad ball. I try to concentrate on the target the whole time, all the way down the approach."[60]

Most bowlers take four or five steps on the approach, though some take as few as three or as many as seven. Most coaches recommend using four steps because they believe it leads to the best timing. As Jowdy explains, "in a four-step delivery, if the pushaway coordinates with the first step, the movement and weight of the ball will develop the proper rhythm."[61] Some elite bowlers, however, prefer taking five or more steps because they find this adds momentum and power to their throws. Other bowlers add power by raising the ball higher on the backswing.

The higher the ball is held during the third step, the more gravitational potential energy will be transferred to the ball.

On the first step, known as the key step, a right-handed bowler steps forward with the right foot and moves the ball forward into the pushaway. Here, he pushes the ball away from the body and ends up holding it in the right hand. Experts say the ideal length of the first step is slightly shorter than the distance the arm is extended in the pushaway. They also recommend taking natural steps, with the heel touch-

Centripetal Force and the Arm Swing

One reason using a ball with the proper weight is important is that a bowler must be able to repeatedly swing the arm in a relaxed, continuously moving arc. If the ball is too heavy, the individual will have to strain to hold it, and the arm muscles will tighten too much to allow a pendulum swing controlled by gravity. The arm swing should involve a smooth, continuous motion because otherwise the ball will fly away at the top of the backswing. This is because a force called the centripetal force keeps the ball on the hand, even with a relaxed grip, as long as the arm keeps moving. The name centripetal comes from the Latin words *centrum* (meaning center) and *petere* (meaning to seek). This "center-seeking" force pulls a rotating object toward the center of the circular path on which it rotates and therefore keeps it on that path.

Bowling coach Michelle Mullen writes in her book *Bowling Fundamentals* that many of her students grip the ball too tightly because they are afraid they will fling it backward. Mullen has these students perform an experiment where they place a nickel on an open palm and swing the arm in a full pendulum swing. She finds that the students are amazed that the nickel stays on the open palm if the swing motion is continuous and has enough momentum.

ing the ground before the toes do, to maintain the best balance. During the key step, the knees extend and the hips flex as the bowler shifts his weight slightly forward, with the chest remaining upright to help with balance.

On the second step, the arm holding the ball begins to swing downward and ends up straight down next to the person's side. The knees are slightly bent, and the step is slightly longer than the first step. The body weight is distributed over the legs, with the large quadriceps muscles providing most of the leverage and balance.

The third step, known as the power step, starts by pushing off from the ball of the foot rather than the heel to help push the body into the fourth step, or slide. The third step is also slightly longer or faster than the second step to increase the momentum and power that goes into the slide. The knees bend more on the third step as well to help with balance. During the third step, the swing arm goes way back into the backswing, while the opposite arm extends out to the side to provide balance. The swing arm should be straight out behind the body, between the shoulders and the waist. The higher back the ball is held, the more force will be transferred to it because of gravitational potential energy. Coaches emphasize that the entire arm swing should be relaxed, allowing the force of gravity, rather than muscle force, to move the arm and the ball. A relaxed arm swing works like a clock pendulum. When the arm swings freely backward and forward with the same force in a pendulum-like motion, this allows consistent shots. Since the force of gravity is consistent, allowing gravity to power the motion is the best way of bowling consistently.

The Final Step and Ball Delivery

During the fourth step, the arm swings down, letting gravity pull the ball down for the release at the bottom of the arc, where the ball is next to the ankle of the sliding foot. The thumb slides out of the thumbhole, followed by the fingers exiting the finger holes. Experts say the position of the fingers and thumb is critical just before and during the release. "The most important component in a great release is the position of the thumb and fingers PRIOR to the release point. . . . [T]he degree of rotation a bowler desires is contingent on the position of the thumb in relation to the palm. The further the thumb moves away from the palm, the greater the rotation,"[62] according to Jowdy in an article in *Bowling This Month*.

While the swing arm heads downward on the fourth step, the opposite arm extends upward or remains extended to the side, depending on individual preference, to help with balance. Then, the swing arm follows through after releasing the ball. The follow-through is a critical element of the ball delivery. It influences power, consistency, and the bowler's balance. A good follow-through includes an extended arm that barely bends and that goes outward, rather than upward, in line with the body's lineup towards the target. If the arm extends upward, this results in the ball spinning in the air and bouncing on the lane, so it loses momentum and also tends to hook too early.

The footwork on the slide is also important. The reason for sliding on the last step is that the bowler's momentum would be lost if he simply stopped at the foul line. Researchers at the National Chung Hsing University in Taiwan found in a 2102 study that the slide also contributes to lower body stability. "The ability to slide the foot consistently enables the bowler to have a predictable stable base from which to deliver the ball more accurately,"[63] the researchers wrote.

Follow-through at ball delivery improves power, consistency, and the bowler's balance.

Biomechanics Technology

United States Bowling Congress (USBC) scientists developed technology that measures bowlers' grip and foot pressure and transmits the data to a computer. Pressure sensors are attached to a special glove on the bowler's throwing hand and to special pads in his shoes. The grip pressure sensors measure the amount of pressure the bowler puts on various parts of his hand as he grips the ball during the approach and ball delivery. Awareness of this information can help coaches teach bowlers methods of reducing grip pressure to make their releases more efficient. The foot pressure sensors measure how much pressure the feet apply to the floor at various points during the approach and ball release. Research engineer Paul Ridenour, who developed the technology, explains that "Foot pressure provides coaches with important data about a bowler's tempo, consistency of the approach, timing, power step, the slide and posting a shot."

Overall, Ridenour states, the rationale for using these technologies is that "These systems work together with coaching. USBC hopes that by understanding biomechanics and applying these systems to the sport of bowling we can give our coaches the most advanced tools to analyze bowlers and help teach athletes of all ability levels."

Quoted in *Bowling Digital*. "USBC Develops New Biomechanics Technology for Bowling." March 14, 2008. www.bowlingdigital.com/bowl/node/3767.

Going into the slide, the left foot steps directly forward, then slides with the toe hitting the ground, followed by the heel. The right leg extends behind the body at an angle, with the weight on the toe and the heel raised. Keeping this leg at an angle creates torque, which adds even more power to the shot. The further back the back leg stretches, the lower the hips are and the more the knees bend. Many bowlers' knees bend deeply, almost to a sitting position, to store energy that can be transferred to the ball when the leg muscles stretch from the bent position. At the same time, the chest remains upright. Getting into this position requires much flexibility and strength. The deep knee bend also helps the bowler release the ball on a low path so it does not drop abruptly onto the lane. Experts advise bowlers to release the ball at a twenty to twenty-five degree angle with the lane so it moves forward and lands gradually like an airplane lands, rather than dropping straight down.

Timing and Release Errors

Many bowlers initially make the mistake of dropping the ball onto the lane rather than launching it on a low, smooth path. Often, this is because the bowler releases the ball too soon, before it is next to the ankle of the front leg. In addition to damaging the lane, bowling champion and coach Ron Clifton explains that "When the ball is released from a high altitude it crashes into the lane like a dumb bomb with much of its forward momentum and revs going into the lane instead of *down* the lane. This is a waste of valuable energy that is lost on the lane surface instead of on the pins."[64] Many coaches recommend overcoming this problem by placing a towel just beyond the foul line and aiming to project the ball past the towel so it follows a more gradual descent. Clifton uses another teaching method—his Multifunctional Optimal Positioner technique. He places a chair in one lane gutter and partly in the next lane's gutter. Then he places a mop with its long handle over the lane. The object is to throw the ball under the mop handle. He jokingly calls the mop he uses a "Multifunctional Optimal Positioner (MOP)."[65]

Another common error is that many bowlers neglect to perform a complete arm follow-through after releasing the ball. Baginski explains, "If you cut the follow through short, or have no follow through, the ball will hook early and have no finish, or no drive when it hits the pins. Follow through imparts rotation on the ball, and rotation translates into ball hitting power."[66]

Other frequent errors occur with coordinating the timing on the arm swing and legwork. In early timing, the ball usually swings ahead of the body, rather than straight down, on the second step. This often happens because the bowler pushes the ball downward on the pushaway or because the key step is too long. The reason for too large a step is often that the bowler started too far behind the foul line. Early timing can lead a bowler to release the ball too early, with his shoulder well forward of the opposite knee. This will result in a throw with less power because the body lacks a fully leveraged position.

Late timing on the approach occurs when the bowler begins the arm swing too late. The ball remains in front of the body, rather than down at the bowler's side, on the second step. This usually happens when the individual pushes the ball upward rather than outward on the push-away or when the swing elbow locks, preventing the arm from dropping down. Taking a key step that is too small can also result in late timing because it does not allow enough time for the bowler to move the arm where it should move. When a bowler's timing on the slide step is late, he will release the ball too late, so the throw will not be as accurate.

Timing errors also occur when bowlers try to transfer power from the swing arm's muscles to the ball instead of relying on the legs to generate this power. This disrupts the continuous pendulum swing motion and therefore interferes with the timing of the arm and leg coordination. This can result in an early or late ball release.

Bowling Styles

Coordinating the footwork and arm motions during the approach and ball release are not the only factors that affect the quality of a bowling shot. The wrist and finger motions that impart spin to the ball when it is released also influence power and accuracy. Bowling experts have divided bowlers into four categories, depending on the type of release they practice. Although most bowlers do not use one style exclusively, they are usually referred to by the category that fits most of their shots.

The first category is power players, also called crankers, who apply force to the ball by rotating the wrist counter-clockwise (for a right-handed player), with the middle and ring fingers placed between the eight o'clock and eleven o'clock positions during the backswing and rotating at the release to give the ball a high rev rate. Power players are known for generating more revolutions than other bowlers. This makes them "cover more boards on the lane, sacrifice accuracy, widen the angle to the pocket, and rely on the ball's explosive contact with the pins,"[67] according to Jowdy.

Walter Ray Williams Jr. releases the ball during the 2003 PBA Championship. Williams—the all-time record holder for the most PBA Tour titles—is a stroker who also successfully uses the end-over-end technique.

Balancing Power and Accuracy

Professional bowler Robert Smith is known as a power player who delivers a fast ball with a wide hook. When Smith was a collegiate player at San Diego State University, coach John Jowdy suggested that he obtain better control of the ball's accuracy by reducing the intensity of his arm follow-through after releasing the ball. Smith improved to the point of being selected for Team USA.

However, after Smith began bowling professionally he had difficulties controlling the wide hook he imparted to the ball. This time, Jowdy determined that fine-tuning his grip on the ball would help resolve the problem. Jowdy recommended that Smith have his bowling balls drilled with more of a forward pitch in the ring finger hole to reduce the amount this finger rotated. This allowed Smith to maintain the power he put into the ball, while reducing the amount of side rotation on the ball. The adjustments helped Smith win five championships, illustrating how bowling well involves complex interactions between biomechanics, technique, and bowling equipment.

The second category of bowlers, strokers, or tweeners, apply fewer revolutions to the ball and tend to bowl more accurately than power players. The ball enters the pocket at a less extreme angle than one thrown by a power player, thus increasing accuracy. Strokers achieve their goals by using a relaxed pendulum arm swing, balancing power and finesse. They therefore tend to consistently win championships.

The wrists of spinners, the third type of bowler, make a spinning motion that leads the fingers to end up on top of the ball when it is released. This makes the ball grip the lane less, so spinner shots are ineffective on oily lanes. They are, however, very effective on dry lanes. Most elite bowlers are not spinners, but those who are, such as Tom Baker, do well with this technique. The main advantage of spinning is that the ball hooks further down the lane and can pack a great deal of power when it hits the pocket.

Bowlers who fit into the fourth category use the end-over-end technique that gives the ball the maximum forward roll and very little side roll. To achieve this type of roll, end-over-enders release the ball with little or no finger rotation. According to Jowdy in a *Bowling This Month* article, "An end-over-end shot requires deadly accuracy coupled with sufficient speed . . . [but] is the simplest shot for controlling the ball's path to the pocket."[68] Professional bowler Walter Ray Williams, who has set records for winning PBA titles, is the best-known champion who successfully uses the end-over-end method.

Many bowlers wish to change their release method to improve their scores, but as former PBA champion and coach Rich Carruba writes in an article on the Bowlingball website, doing so is not a simple matter: "Adding revs to your bowling ball and changing the axis tilt to promote a sharper angle of entry on the back end of the lane requires physical changes in your game other than hand action. Changing your footwork pattern and your swing path alignment also are important to match with a new release style."[69]

Indeed, the interactions among the factors which contribute to good bowling are complex, and making positive changes can involve complex adjustments. Many top bowlers do well because of their ability to quickly adapt to changing lane conditions by using a variety of hand positions and rotations. According to a *Bowling This Month* article,

Although many PBA players have mastered proper speed control to overcome diverse lane conditions, those who also possess the art of alternating hand positions enjoy a distinct advantage over those who rely principally on powerful deliveries. Chris Barnes and Norm Duke exemplify versatility by virtue of their innate ability to alter hand positions at any given opportunity. The late Earl Anthony, who collected 41 titles, never relied on an overpowering strike ball, yet he compensated for this by applying proper hand positions, changing speeds, and displaying unerring accuracy.[70]

The down side of the countless practice sessions and games involved in learning and perfecting the proper arm swing, wrist and hand rotations, and footwork is that the repeated motions can be hard on the muscles and other body structures that power these movements. Indeed, bowlers sustain many more injuries than most people imagine.

CHAPTER **7**

Sports Medicine and Bowling

W hile bowling is not known for causing the serious injuries that occur in many sports, bowlers do experience a variety of injuries from overuse or misuse of muscles and other body parts. The field of medicine that diagnoses and treats all types of sports injuries is called sports medicine. Any medical doctor can diagnose and treat sports injuries, but those who only treat sports injuries are known as sports medicine specialists. Orthopedic surgeons, who are specially trained to perform surgery or otherwise care for bone and muscle injuries and diseases, also treat many sports injuries. Sports medicine specialists work closely with coaches, physical therapists, and other rehabilitation therapists to help athletes prevent injuries and to assist with recovery if the injuries occur.

Many people, including bowlers, are surprised to find out that so many bowling injuries occur because they do not believe bowling is a strenuous sport. For example, in 2012 professional basketball player Andrew Bynum, an avid recreational bowler, told sports-television channel ESPN that he was surprised when he hurt his knee while bowling: "I didn't twist it or fall or nothing. It kind of broke off cartilage and it made the bone bruise bigger."[71] At the time, Bynum was recovering from a bone bruise in his knee, and doctors informed him that bowling had made it worse. Bynum stated that he did not think bowling would hurt his knee any more than the low-impact exercises he was already performing in physical therapy.

Why Injuries Occur

Bowling injuries occur, in part, because "Bowling may not be a physically strenuous activity like other sports that involve running and jumping BUT bowling balls do weigh more than any other ball used in other sports. . . . If you think that doesn't take a toll on your body—THINK AGAIN!"[72] states physical therapist and fitness specialist Heather D'Errico in a 2014 *Bowling Industry News* article. Australian physiotherapist John Miller explains that in addition, "you have a very heavy weight hanging off your fingers that you swing back and forwards before sliding in slippery shoes during your delivery. Plus, you have to lift up that heavy ball many times during a game."[73]

Since many bowling injuries result from overusing certain muscles and joints in conjunction with swinging a heavy ball, experts find that many long-time professional and amateur bowlers who keep grueling competition schedules—many that include bowling more than fifty games per week—are most often affected. For instance, during a string of competitions in 2012, professional bowler Tom Baker suffered unrelenting pain in his calves and toes from pushing off his feet during the ball release. He also had to have wrist surgery. Baker told the *Star-Ledger* newspaper that he and many other professional bowlers take pain medicines regularly. He stated, "It's not like you just get up and bowl and you feel great at the end of the block."[74] Sometimes resting affected muscles and joints or having surgery help alleviate these types of pain, but not always. Some bowlers, such as Don Johnson, are forced to retire because of injuries. In 1999 Johnson retired because a thumb injury would not heal.

Some overuse injuries result from the way in which a particular bowler holds the ball. Professional bowler Amleto Monacelli, for example, gripped the ball with his

Rising Above Injuries

One professional bowler known for his persistence and refusal to let injuries defeat him is Michael Haugen Jr. In a demonstration of his persistence, at the 2008 PBA Tournament of Champions Haugen was down by fifty-three pins in the sixth frame. Refusing to give up, he turned things around with five consecutive strikes and won the tournament, defeating Chris Barnes by one pin. A week later, Haugen tore tendons in his finger while helping children in his hometown of Phoenix, Arizona, learn to bowl. He had to stop bowling for the season, ending his chances of becoming the PBA Player of the Year. During his next season, he tore the anterior cruciate ligament in his knee—a notoriously painful and debilitating injury. He elected not to have surgery, and spent many months resting, recovering, and getting himself back in shape to compete. In 2011 the Internet series called The Pain Channel featured Haugen's story in a video titled *The Heart of A Champion*, noting that his commitment to bowling led him to rise above his injuries to keep competing. Despite lingering pain, Haugen resumed his professional career, winning his third PBA title in 2013 at the Mark Roth Classic Tournament.

pinkie finger on top and his ring finger bearing all the ball's weight. His ring finger tendons ripped and he could not pick up a bowling ball for six months. Other injuries, particularly lower body injuries, happen because of improper technique during the approach to the foul line. For instance, a 2012 study found that "While bowling, the bowler should keep the lower limbs stable to avoid injury. . . . Lower limb injuries are related to the bowler's gait [type of walk] and stance while throwing the ball. An improper gait and/or stance can cause adductor muscle strains, ankle sprains, knee ligament injuries and femoral shaft fractures."[75]

Common Bowling Injuries

A 2011 study by researchers at Ohio State University found that there were about 375,468 bowling injuries reported in the United States between 1990 and 2008. The most common injuries involved the thumb and fingers (19 percent), trunk (15.8 percent), or ankles/feet/toes (14.9 percent). The injuries were commonly strains or sprains (42.7 percent) and soft-tissue injuries (20.3 percent). Children under age seven had the most finger injuries and injuries such as broken feet from dropping a ball on a foot, while seniors over age sixty-five had the most injuries from falling. However, other studies indicate that children are not the only ones who drop bowling balls on their feet. Adults do so as well, and both children and adults occasionally fling or drop the ball during the backswing, which can seriously injure other people.

A more recent U.S. Consumer Product Safety Commission study reported that there were about seventeen thousand bowling injuries in the United States in 2013, based on hospital emergency room treatment records. Some injuries involved lacerations (cuts) and scrapes, as occurred when a man fell and cut his leg on the edge of a bowling lane gutter. Many injuries involved sprains or strains in fingers, wrists, and hands from repeatedly gripping a bowling ball. Some people broke bones in the hands, arms, or legs when they fell down while bowling. Some sustained bruises by hitting the legs with a bowling ball.

The most common injuries, sprains and strains, affect a wide range of body parts. The American Academy of Orthopedic Surgeons (AAOS) explains that "A sprain is caused by direct or indirect trauma (a fall, a blow to the body, etc) that knocks a joint out of position, and overstretches, and, in severe cases, ruptures the supporting ligaments."[76] A strain, on the other hand, involves an injury to a muscle or tendon. While sprains are often acute (sudden) injuries, strains can be acute or chronic

KINGPIN

The thumb is the most commonly injured body part in bowlers.

Bowling and Anti-Doping Rules

Although bowling has not been affected by doping violations as much as many sports have, it has still been touched by these problems. Doping involves using performance-enhancing drugs such as steroids or amphetamines that are not prescribed for a medical condition. Like governing organizations for other sports, the World Tenpin Bowling Association has anti-doping rules that bind all amateur and professional bowlers. These rules were formulated to "preserve what is intrinsically valuable about sport. This intrinsic value is often referred to as 'the spirit of sport'." The "spirit of sport" is characterized by fair play, honesty, dedication, character, and respect for rules.

Any athlete caught using banned drugs and those who refuse to be tested for drugs can be banned from a tournament or even from the sport. In one doping incident in 2005, two members of the British Tenpin Bowling Association Nationals Team England were banned for two years from the Premier Tenpin Bowling Club after testing positive for cocaine. In another incident, in March 2014 the United States Professional Anti-Doping Agency announced that bowler Shannon O'Keefe of Texas tested positive for a prohibited hormone called clomiphene and received a public warning. O'Keefe explained that her physician had prescribed the drug, and that she was not taking it to enhance her performance. She was not punished, but was warned that she needed special permission to take banned substances, even when prescribed by a doctor.

World Tenpin Bowling Association. "Anti-Doping Rules." www.worldtenpinbowling.com/pdf/WTBAAnti DopingRules.pdf.

(long-term). According to AAOS, "Chronic strains are the result of overuse (prolonged, repetitive movement) of muscles and tendons. Inadequate rest breaks during intensive training precipitates a strain. Acute strains are caused by a direct blow to the body, overstretching, or excessive muscle contraction."[77]

Sprains and strains can be mild, moderate, or severe. Mild or moderate sprains and strains often get better with rest, ice, elevation, and compression (enclosure in a fairly tight bandage). Severe sprains or strains involve tearing of the structure, which often results in a great deal of pain and an inability to move the affected muscle or joint. Surgery and many months of rehabilitation are often required to treat severe sprains and strains.

Hand and Wrist Injuries

Many types of bowling injuries, including sprains and strains, are chronic overuse injuries involving the hand and wrist of the swing arm. According to the World of Sports Science website, these injuries are common because during the arm swing,

> the arm and wrist of the bowler are taken through an eccentric motion, where all of the forces of delivery are radiated through the wrist. When the wrist is itself not stable at the time that those forces are received, the tendons of the wrist, which connect the muscles of the forearm to the hand, and the ligaments of the carpal bones of the wrist-joint have the potential to be overstretched; in time, this overstretching can cause a micro-tearing of these connective tissues.[78]

An eccentric motion occurs when a muscle lengthens. Conversely, a concentric motion happens when a muscle contracts.

Some common chronic hand and wrist injuries involve nerve damage as well as connective tissue damage. One common overuse injury is bowler's thumb, also called bowler's neuroma, which usually results from the thumb rubbing repeatedly on the sides of the bowling ball's thumb-hole. Sometimes it affects bowlers who add spin to the ball by not releasing the thumb from the thumbhole until the last possible second. Either way, the injury results from pressure on the ulnar nerve, which runs down the forearm along the ulnar bone, into the hand. The pressure often leads to swelling around the nerve, pain, weakness, and an inability to use the adductor pollicis muscle, which is controlled by the ulnar nerve and which normally moves the thumb toward the center of the hand. According to a study by doctors at the Mayo Clinic in Arizona, reported in the journal *Hand*, "While the incidence of bowler's thumb is unknown, it is an unrelenting nuisance for bowlers, and symptoms

Many common injuries in bowling result from the chronic overuse of the hand and wrist.

can be severe enough to prevent further sport participation."[79] Sometimes having the bowling ball holes re-drilled or using a thumb guard or tape helps this condition. Most of the time, doctors recommend that people with bowler's thumb take a break from bowling until it heals. However, some people need surgery because the injury does not heal on its own. In 2009 the Mayo Clinic doctors developed a new surgical procedure called digital nerve translocation to treat bowler's thumb because "the increased need for competitive bowlers to minimize the time away from the sport dictates a need for a definitive, quick, and successful treatment,"[80] according to their study. The procedure involves cutting the adductor pollicis muscle and re-attaching it to

BOWLER'S THUMB

Bowler's thumb results from the inside of the thumb rubbing repeatedly against the bowling ball's thumb hole, which can cause swelling of the ulnar nerve and loss of control of the adductor pollicis muscle.

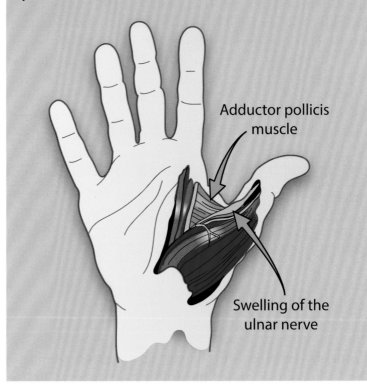

Adductor pollicis muscle

Swelling of the ulnar nerve

the ulnar nerve. The first patient who underwent the surgery was able to resume bowling within about five months, which was much sooner than with previous procedures.

Another common bowling injury that involves nerve compression is carpal tunnel syndrome. This is a wrist injury caused by repeated stress on the median nerve, which runs from the forearm to the palm of the hand, through the carpal tunnel, which is a narrow passageway composed of ligaments, tendons, and bones at the base of the hand. Oftentimes, tendons in the tunnel become inflamed from repetitive actions, and this narrows the tunnel and presses on the nerve. Tingling, numbness, shooting pain, and weakness are typical symptoms. Doctors usually prescribe special exercises or medications injected into the wrist, but if these measures do not alleviate pain, surgery known as carpal tunnel release surgery may be needed. The surgery enlarges the tunnel to relieve pressure on the median nerve.

Another wrist injury called de Quervain's syndrome, or tenosynovitis, also comes from repeatedly holding and throwing a bowling ball. This injury comes from inflammation in tendons in the abductor pollicis longus and extensor pollicis breves muscles in the thumb. It involves pain and swelling in the thumb side of the wrist. Treating the injury early on with ice, rest, immobilization with a splint, special exercises and/or medications to reduce swelling usually results in healing, but occasionally surgery is needed.

Other Bowling Injuries

Another common chronic injury is bowler's arthritis in the knees, wrists, shoulders, or fingers. It often occurs after someone bowls for many years. Bowler's arthritis involves swollen, stiff, painful joints. There are several forms of arthritis, with the most common being osteoarthritis. Osteoarthritis is characterized by cartilage degeneration in the joints and often includes the growth of bone spurs. Doctors state that although anyone can develop osteoarthritis, bowlers who use improper form or who use too heavy a ball are most at risk.

Knee sprains, strains, and other injuries are also common, with most occurring when a bowler's body is balanced over bent knees during the ball release. The knee joint is composed of the femur, fibula, tibia, and patella bones. The patella, or kneecap, moves up and down in a groove on the femur (thigh bone). Repeated knee bends can result in misalignment of the patella, and when this happens, the patella

Most knee injuries occur when a bowler's body is balanced over bent knees during the ball release.

can grind against the femur, causing pain. The four major ligaments that stabilize the knee joint—the medial collateral ligament (MCL), lateral collateral ligament (LCL), anterior cruciate ligament (ACL), and posterior cruciate ligament (PCL)—are also susceptible to being strained or torn from the sudden or repetitive movements that occur in bowling. Most knee injuries in bowlers involve the ACL, which is attached to the back of the femur and tibia. The ACL limits how much the knee joint can rotate. ACL injuries are extremely painful and can take many months to heal, with or without surgery.

Many bowlers develop acute or chronic back injuries as well. Bowlers may strain the back by improperly lifting the ball using only the swing arm, or from muscle fatigue after prolonged bowling. Back injuries often include ligament strains in the muscles around the lumbar vertebrae (bones in the lower back) or problems with the discs between the vertebrae. Discs are rubbery pads that sit between the bones in the spine. They function as shock absorbers for the spine and prevent vertebrae from rubbing against each other. Discs tend to harden as people age, and this makes them prone to herniating (swelling and pushing through the outer covering) or to breaking apart. Either way, inflamed discs can press against the spinal cord or nerves that surround the vertebrae, resulting in excruciating pain. The pain often radiates to the arms or legs, making movement difficult. Many people with disc problems benefit from surgery or from spinal injections that reduce swelling.

Preventing Injuries

Because bowling injuries can be extremely painful and can derail competitive bowling careers, sports medicine experts recommend many preventive measures to help avoid these injuries. One important measure is warming up and stretching before bowling. An ongoing fitness and conditioning program can also help. Another preventive measure is wearing hand, elbow, and wrist guards to support muscles in these areas. Properly picking up the ball with two hands, with the weight being borne by the legs and hips rather than the back, is also important. Using the right ball that is not too heavy and that has holes drilled to fit an individual's

Wearing the correct right-handed or left-handed bowling shoes is crucial to prevent slipping accidents on bowling lanes.

Bowling and Disabilities

Many people with various disabilities enjoy bowling. For example, according to the International Blind Sports Federation, "Tenpin bowling is very popular among the blind."[1] Blind people bowl in regular bowling centers throughout the world. They often require assistance lining up in front of the foul line. Some use guide rails installed in some bowling alleys for this purpose. The rails are held in place with bowling balls placed at the base. After the first roll, sighted assistants tell blind bowlers which pins were knocked down so they can formulate their strategy for the next roll.

People with other sorts of physical and intellectual disabilities also enjoy bowling. The sport first became popular among veterans with disabilities such as limb amputations and paraplegia after World War II in the late 1940s, and has been especially popular since the first wheelchair bowling was introduced into the National Wheelchair Games in 1957. Bowling has been part of the Special Olympics since 1975. The Association of Children's Prosthetic-Orthotic Clinics states that "Today, bowling is one of the most popular indoor sports for the handicapped. This is especially true because the game can be played with some degree of success by almost everyone, regardless of the extent of physical disability."[2]

1. International Blind Sports Federation. "Tenpin Bowling—General Information." www.ibsasport.org/sports/tenpin-bowling.

2. Ronald C. Adams. "Bowling for the Physically Handicapped." The Association of Children's Prosthetic-Orthotic Clinics. www.acpoc.org/library/1970_01_009.asp.

hand is critical in preventing injuries, as bowlers who use poorly fitting balls often end up with finger and thumb abrasions, wrist injuries, and painful joints. Experts also stress the importance of insuring that shoes are clean and free from oil or other substances on the bottom that can make an individual slip and fall. Wearing the correct shoes for a right-handed or left-handed individual is also important for preventing falls. Bowling shoes have a slippery sole on the shoe worn on the bowler's sliding foot to help with the slide. The other shoe has a rippled sole that grips the floor.

One well-known incident in 1983 and other similar incidents have made the public aware that renting and wearing the wrong bowling shoes can be hazardous. Indeed, this is why most serious bowlers purchase custom-made shoes. In 1983, then-future United States president George H.W. Bush went bowling in Milwaukee, Minnesota, and was given a pair of right-handed shoes even though he was left-handed. At the foul line, Bush's right shoe gripped the floor instead of sliding and he went flying into the ground, landing face-first.

A Lifetime Sport

Despite the variety of injuries associated with bowling, sports medicine experts say that bowlers experience far fewer and less severe injuries than those seen in most sports. Indeed, studies show that even with overuse injuries from years of bowling, most bowlers can continue the sport well into middle and old age with minimal declines in performance. A study by researchers at the University of Texas, for example, found that performance in elite bowlers did not begin declining until age forty-five, and even after that age, average bowling scores declined only about eight percent between age twenty and age fifty. The researchers concluded that "This magnitude of decline is considerably smaller than that seen in other athletic events."[81]

This is one reason for the continuing popularity of bowling as a universal sport, which families, friends, and competitors of all ages can enjoy together. Although the sport has changed a great deal over the centuries, experts believe people will continue to flock to bowling lanes for fun and competition. As Parker Bohn III writes, "People have always relished the challenge of attempting to topple objects with an accurately tossed projectile. That should continue for as long as people inhabit the earth."[82]

Chapter 1: Bowling: A Game for All

1. Max Gross. "The Heritage of American Ten Pins." *American Ten Pins.* www.americantenpins.com/PartOne.htm.

2. International Bowling Museum and Hall of Fame. "History of Bowling." www.bowlingmuseum.com/Visit/HistoryofBowling.aspx.

3. J. Bruce Pluckhahn. "Bowling." *Encyclopedia Britannica*, December 14, 2014. www.britannica.com/EBchecked/topic/76233/bowling.

4. Quoted in Daniel Diehl and Mark Donnelly. *Medieval Celebrations.* Mechanicsburg, PA: Stackpole Books, 2011, p. 111.

5. Gross. "The Heritage of American Ten Pins."

6. Quoted in Johnny Acton, Tania Adams, and Matt Packer. *Origin of Everyday Things.* New York: Sterling, 2006, p. 35.

7. Quoted in Gross. "The Heritage of American Ten Pins."

8. Parker Bohn III. *Bowling: How to Master the Game.* New York: Universe, 2000, p. 13.

9. Pluckhahn. "Bowling."

10. Bohn. *Bowling: How to Master the Game*, p. 20.

11. Earl Hunsinger, "Bowling: The Sport of Kings and Working Men." Buzzle, April 4, 2008. www.buzzle.com/articles/bowling-the-sport-of-kings-and-working-men.html.

Chapter 2: Physics and Bowling

12. Rice University Teacher Tech. "First Law of Motion." http://teachertech.rice.edu/Participants/louviere/Newton/law1.html.

13. Jim Lucas. "Equal and Opposite Reactions: Newton's Third Law of Motion." *Live Science*, June 26, 2014. www.livescience.com/46561-newton-third-law.html.

14. Giuseppe Gozzi. "The Physics of Bowling." June 15, 2013. http://prezi.com/rji0vz5fvqnp/copy-of-the-physics-of-bowling/.

15. Institute of Physics. "Episode 214: Work Done By A Force." http://tap.iop.org/mechanics/wep/214/page_46390.html.

16. Gozzi. "The Physics of Bowling."

17. John Eric Goff. *Gold Medal Physics: The Science of Sports.* Baltimore:

The Johns Hopkins University Press, 2010, p. 22.

18. Ron McIntosh. *Bowler's Handbook: A Guide to Almost Everything in Bowling*. Elfers, FL: McIntosh, 2006, p. 45.

19. Ruth W. Chabay and Bruce A. Sherwood. *Matter and Interactions*. Hoboken, NJ: John Wiley & Sons, 2011, p. 384.

Chapter 3: Biomechanics and Bowling

20. Carol A. Oatis. *Kinesiology: The Mechanics and Pathomechanics of Human Movement*, 2nd ed. Baltimore: Lippincott Williams & Wilkins, 2009, p. 3.

21. Oatis, *Kinesiology: The Mechanics and Pathomechanics of Human Movement*, 2nd ed., p. 45.

22. Tom Benson. "First Law of Thermodynamics." National Aeronautics and Space Administration, June 12, 2014. www.grc.nasa.gov/WWW/k-12/airplane/thermo1.html.

23. National Institutes of Health. "Nutrition and Athletic Performance." www.nlm.nih.gov/medlineplus/ency/article/002458.htm.

24. James Knierim. "Chapter 1: Motor Units and Muscle Receptors." Neuroscience Online, University of Texas Medical School. http://neuroscience.uth.tmc.edu/s3/chapter01.html.

25. National Council on Strength and Fitness. "How Does Velocity Affect

Force and Power." www.ncsf.org/enew/articles/articles-velocityandpower.aspx.

26. National Council on Strength and Fitness. "How Does Velocity Affect Force and Power."

27. Stanley P. Brown, Wayne C. Miller, and M. Eason. *Exercise Physiology: Basis of Human Movement in Health and Disease*. Baltimore, MD: Lippincott Williams & Wilkins, 2006, p. 277.

28. Bruce Abernethy, Vaughan Kippers, Stephanie Hanrahan, Marcus Pandy, Ali McManus, and Laurel Mackinnon. *Biophysical Foundations of Human Movement*, 3rd ed. South Melbourne, Victoria, Australia: Macmillan Education Australia, 2013, p. 116.

29. Quoted in Bohn. *Bowling: How to Master the Game*, p. 99.

Chapter 4: The Mental Game

30. Michelle Mullen. *Bowling Fundamentals*, 2nd ed. Champaign, IL: Human Kinetics, 2014, p. 191.

31. Dean Hinitz. *Focused for Bowling*. Champaign, IL: Human Kinetics, 2003, p. 2.

32. Quoted in Bohn. *Bowling: How To Master the Game*, p. 78.

33. Hinitz. *Focused for Bowling*, p. 8.

34. JoAnn Dahlkoetter. "Mental Toughness Training: Create Your Own Inner Fire." DrJoAnn.com, September 11, 2009. www.drjoann.com/tough/.

35. Mullen. *Bowling Fundamentals,* p. x.
36. Earl Anthony. *Winning Bowling.* Chicago: Contemporary Books, 1977, p. 46.
37. Jim Taylor. "Sport Imagery: Athletes' Most Powerful Mental Tool." *Psychology Today,* November 6, 2012. www.psychologytoday.com /blog/the-power-prime/201211 /sport-imagery-athletes-most -powerful-mental-tool.
38. JoAnn Dahlkoetter. "The Virtual Workout: Using Positive Imagery." www.sports-psych.com/articles _02.html.
39. John Jowdy. *Bowling Execution.* Champaign, IL: Human Kinetics, 2009, p. 3.
40. Quoted in Mike Jasnau. "How to Direct Young Players, Developing Strong Mental Attitudes in Youth, and Dispelling Bad Attitudes at the Adult Level." *Bowling This Month,* August 14, 2014. www.bowling thismonth.com/article/coaching -discussion/.
41. Mullen. *Bowling Fundamentals,* p. 194.
42. Quoted in Jasnau. "How to Direct Young Players."
43. Anthony. *Winning Bowling,* p. 141.
44. William Powers and Robert Strickland. *Bowling Tough.* Everett, WA: Robert H. Strickland and Associates, 2007, p. 24.
45. Quoted in Action Bowlers. "Johnny Petraglia." www.actionbowlers.com /action/petraglia.htm.
46. Quoted in George Dohrmann. "He Cuts Familiar, Striking Figure." *Los Angeles Times,* March 6, 1996. http://articles.latimes.com/1996 -03-06/sports/sp-43656_1_mike -aulby.
47. Hinitz. *Focused for Bowling,* p. 104.
48. Powers and Strickland. *Bowling Tough,* p. 27.

Chapter 5: Pre-Throw Strategies

49. Mike Aulby, Dave Ferraro, and Dan Herbst. *Bowling 200+: Winning Strategies to Up Your Average and Improve Your Game.* Chicago: Contemporary Books, 1989, p. 1.
50. Mullen. *Bowling Fundamentals,* p. 6.
51. Neil Stremmel. "Entry Angle, Part 1." http://wiki.bowlingchat.net/wi ki/images/c/c6/Entry_Angle_By _Neil_Stremmel.pdf.
52. Neil Stremmel. "Entry Angle, Part 3." http://wiki.bowlingchat .net/wiki/images/c/c6/Entry _Angle_By_Neil_Stremmel.pdf.
53. Anthony. *Winning Bowling,* p. 50.
54. United States Bowling Congress. "Preparing for a Tournament." www.bowl.com/Coaching /Coaching_Features/Interme diate/.
55. Anthony. *Winning Bowling,* p. 97.
56. Jowdy. *Bowling Execution,* p. 16.
57. Michael Haugen Jr. "Blogs— WSOB V." October 30, 2013. www .michaelhaugenjr.com/blog.
58. Quoted in Aulby, Ferraro, and Herbst. *Winning Strategies,* p. 1.

Chapter 6: Coordinating Physics and Bio-mechanics

59. Mullen. *Bowling Fundamentals*, p. 17.
60. Quoted in McIntosh. *Bowler's Handbook*, p. 6.
61. Jowdy. *Bowling Execution*, p. 55.
62. John Jowdy. "Bowling by the Clock: Hand Positions by the Numbers." *Bowling This Month*, October 17, 2014. www.bowling thismonth.com/article/bowling -by-the-clock/.
63. Chung-Shun Hung, Li-Cheng Hsieh, and Hong-Wen Wu. "Development of a Simple Force Prediction Model and Consistency Assessment of Knee Movements in Ten-Pin Bowling." *Maejo International Journal of Science Technology* vol. 6, no. 2 (2012): p. 298.
64. Ron Clifton. "A Smooth Landing (Part 1)." *Bowler Central*, July 7, 2007. http://bowlercentral.com/Ro nClifton.htm#RonNews28.
65. Ron Clifton. "A Smooth Landing (Part 1).
66. Quoted in McIntosh, *Bowler's Handbook*, p. 8.
67. Jowdy. *Bowling Execution*, p. 49.
68. John Jowdy. "Changing Hand Positions: The Key Remedy for Overcoming Lane Conditions." *Bowling This Month*, September 19, 2014. www.bowlingthismonth.com/ar ticle/changing-hand-positions/.
69. Rich Carruba. "How to Change Bowling Hand Positions." Bowling ball.com. www.bowlingball.com /BowlVersity/how-to-change -bowling-hand-positions.
70. Jowdy. "Changing Hand Positions."

Chapter 7: Sports Medicine and Bowling

71. Quoted in Brian Windhorst. "Andrew Bynum: 'Got to Bide Time.'" ESPN, November 19, 2012. http:// espn.go.com/nba/story/_/id /8649876/andrew-bynum-injury -bowling-not-more-strenuous -rehab.
72. Heather D'Errico. "Does Physical Training Affect the Biomechanics of Bowling?" *Bowling Industry News*, March 3, 2014. http://storm bowling.com/news/2014/03/4407.
73. John Miller. "Ten Pin Bowling Injuries." *Physioworks*. www.physio works.com.au/Injuries-conditions /Activities/ten-pin-bowling-in juries.
74. Quoted in Conor Orr. "PBA Bowlers Face the Danger of Injuries Thanks to Grueling Competitive Schedule." *Star-Ledger*, February 23, 2012. www.nj.com/sports /index.ssf/2012/02/pba_bowlers _face_the_danger_of.html.
75. Chung-Shun Hung et al. "Development of a Simple Force Prediction Model," p. 298.
76. American Academy of Orthopedic Surgeons. "Sprains and Strains: What's the Difference?" http://orthoinfo.aaos.org/topic .cfm?topic=A00111.

77. American Academy of Orthopedic Surgeons. "Sprains and Strains: What's the Difference?"

78. World of Sports Science. "Bowling." http://www.faqs.org/sports-science/Ba-Ca/Bowling.html.

79. Scott Swanson, Luis H. Macias, and Anthony A. Smith. "Treatment of Bowler's Neuroma with Digital Nerve Translocation." *Hand* vol. 4, no. 3 (September 2009): p. 323.

80. Swanson et al. "Treatment of Bowler's Neuroma." p. 323.

81. Allison Elizabeth DeVan and Hirofumi Tanaka. "Declines in Ten-Pin Bowling Performance with Advancing Age." *Age and Ageing* vol. 36, no. 6 (2007): p. 694.

82. Bohn. *Bowling: How To Master the Game*, p. 35.

GLOSSARY

acceleration: The amount an object speeds up

biomechanics: The study of how the laws of physics and mechanics affect how the human body moves

breakpoint: The farthest point out on the lane a bowling ball goes before it hooks toward the pins

core: The interior of a bowling ball

coverstock: The outer covering of a bowling ball

force: A source of energy that pushes or pulls an object

gravity: The force that pulls objects to the earth's surface

hook: A curved path on which a bowling ball rolls

inertia: The tendency of an object at rest to remain at rest or an object in motion to remain in constant motion

kinesiology: The science that studies movement

kinetic: Referring to motion

kingpin: The five-pin, which is the most important pin to hit to achieve a strike

leverage: Power generated by pressing a body part against the ground

ligament: Cartilage that connects bones to each other

loft: The path of a bowling ball in the air right after it is released

mass: A measurement of how much matter an object contains

momentum: A measurement of the direction and speed of a moving object as it relates to its mass

myocytes: Muscle cells

physics: The science that describes and explains the properties and relationships between physical objects

pitch: The angle at which the holes are drilled into a bowling ball

pocket: The space between two of the front-most pins for which bowlers aim

power: The amount of force exerted in a given amount of time

span: The distance from the finger holes to the thumbhole on a bowling ball

spare: Knocking down all the bowling pins in two turns

split: A gap between two remaining bowling pins after the first throw

sprain: An overstretched or torn ligament

strain: An injury to a muscle or tendon

strike: Knocking down all ten bowling pins on the first try

tendon: Cartilage that connects muscles to bones

torque: A measurement of how much force acting on an object causes the object to rotate

velocity: A measurement of how fast an object is changing its original position

FOR MORE INFORMATION

Books

Michelle Mullen. *Bowling Fundamentals*, 2nd ed. Champaign, IL: Human Kinetics, 2014. This book aims to help bowlers improve their game. It discusses all aspects of bowling skills and some of the science behind how and why certain techniques work best.

Gail Stewart. *Sports Medicine Research*. San Diego, CA: ReferencePoint, 2012. This book for teens examines research that seeks to better understand, prevent, and treat all types of sports injuries.

Articles

Keith Oliver. "Bowling the In-School Way (with Lessons for Math and Science)." www.okaloosaschools.com /shalimar/sites/okaloosaschools .com.shalimar/files/users/gilll/Bowl ing%20Book.pdf. This article discusses bowling history, techniques, and the science behind bowling.

Topendsports. "The Physics of Bowling." www.topendsports.com/sport /tenpin/physics.htm. This article discusses the physics concepts that underlie bowling.

Videos

ESPN Video: *Sport Science: PBA's Sean Rash* (http://espn.go.com/vid eo/clip?id=10767943). ESPN commentators place sensors on elite bowler Sean Rash to help illustrate the biomechanics and physics that underlie Rash's bowling moves in a video from April 11, 2014.

HEC-TV Live: *The Science Behind Bowling* (www.hectv.org/vid eo/14207/the-science-behind-bow ling).This video explains the physics underlying bowling, including concepts such as forces, friction, gravity, and Newton's laws of motion.

Inside Science TV: *Bowling Robot Shows How to Throw More Strikes* (www.insidescience.org/content /bowling-robot-shows-how-throw -more-strikes/816.) In a video from October 16, 2012, a robot named EARL shows how different lane surfaces and bowling styles affect bowling ball motion and bowler success.

INDEX

A

Acceleration, 24–25, 27–28, 30–31
Adenosine triphosphate, 41–42, 45
Age of bowlers, 107
Albert Edward, Prince, 13
American Bowling Congress, 14–15, 20
Angular momentum, 36–37
Angular velocity, 45–46
Anthony, Earl, 93
Anti-doping rules, 99
Approach, *40*, 83–86, *84*, 88–90
Aristotle, 41
Arm swing, 84–87, 90
Arthritis, 103
ATP, 41–42, 45
Automatic pinsetters, *17*, 17–18

B

Back injuries, 104–105
Balance, 49
Ball delivery, 86–89, *87*, 93
Balls. *See* Bowling balls
Barnes, Chris, 93
Bates, Sully, 19
Bernoulli's principle, 29
Biomechanics
    approach, 83–86
    Aristotle, 41
    ball delivery, 86–89
    flexibility, 49–50
    motor units, 43–45
    muscles, 39–42, 45–46

strength and power, 46–48
technology, 88
Boards, 79–80
Bowler's thumb, 100–102, *102*
Bowling balls, 18–21, *19*, 33, 68–72, *69*, 105–106
Breakpoint, 79–80
Bumper bowling, 16
Burnout, 65–67, *66*
Bush, George H.W., 107

C

Cardiovascular fitness, 51
Careers in sports science, 43
Carpal tunnel syndrome, 102–103
Celebrities, 13, 14
Centripetal force, 85
Charity, 13
Clothing, 51
Collisions, 37–38
Comedians, 13
Concentration. *See* Focus
Confidence, 56
Conservation of momentum, 37–38
Coordination, 49

D

De Quervain's syndrome, 103
Determination, 64
Diet and nutrition, *42*, 43
Disabled persons, 106
Doping, 99
Drag, 29

PICTURE CREDITS

Cover: © Anton Balazh/Shutterstock
.com, © Nejron Photo/Shutterstock
.com, and © Tereshchenko Dmitry/
Shutterstock.com
© 4x6/iStock, 40
© andresrimaging/iStock, 30
© Andy Crawford/Getty Images, 47
© Andy Cross/The Denver Post via
Getty Images, 104
© AP Images/John F. Martin, 91
© Best View Stock/Alamy, 37
© colorftime/iStock, 25
© Corbis, 15
© Cultura RM/Chris Cole/Getty Im-
ages, 50
© Fox Photos/Getty Images, 17
© Fox Photos/Hulton Archive/Getty
Images, 19
© Gale, Cengage Learning, 22, 35, 45,
73, 102

© gilaxia/iStock, 83, 84, 87
© g-stockstudio/iStock, 71
© Hyoung Chang/The Denver Post via
Getty Images, 62
© imageBROKER/Alamy, 101
© Maximilian Stock Ltd./Getty Im-
ages, 42
© pio3/Shutterstock.com, 12
© The Print Collector/Hulton Archive/
Getty Images, 10
© Ryan McVay/Getty Images, 69
© Simon McComb Photography/Getty
Images, 77
© skynesher/iStock, 55, 66, 105
© Sylvia Serrado/Getty Images, 80
© tarasov_vl/iStock, 27
© tomas kraus/Alamy, 72
© Toni L. Sandys/The Washington
Post via Getty Images, 58
© wolv/iStock, 36

ABOUT THE AUTHOR

Melissa Abramovitz has been a freelance writer for nearly thirty years and specializes in writing nonfiction magazine articles and books for all age groups. She is the author of hundreds of magazine articles, more than forty educational books for children and teenagers, numerous poems and short stories, several children's picture books, and a book for writers. Melissa is a graduate of the University of California San Diego and the Institute of Children's Literature. Visit her website at www.melissaabramovitz.com.